WHERE THE SEA STANDS STILL
大海停止之處

Where the Sea Stands Still

NEW POEMS

大海停止之處

新詩集

YANG LIAN

楊煉

TRANSLATED BY

Brian Holton

BLOODAXE BOOKS

ISBN: 978 1 85224 471 2

First published 1999 by
Bloodaxe Books Ltd,
Eastburn,
South Park,
Hexham,
Northumberland NE46 1BS.

This is a digital reprint of the 1999 edition.

www.bloodaxebooks.com

For further information about Bloodaxe titles
please visit our website and join our mailing list
or write to the above address for a catalogue.

Supported using public funding by

ARTS COUNCIL
ENGLAND

Thanks are due to Arts Council England
for providing a translation grant for this book.

Digital reprint by Lightning Source.

CONTENTS

目錄

DARKNESSES

黑暗們

春天，或在你的愛裡有一條河的疼痛

在你的目光裡有一隻鳥最明亮的恐怖
在你的愛裡有一條河的疼痛

一個被打碎的日子　讓你躲不開
這堆滿雪白冰塊的河床
筆記本密集發芽的視野中
每棵樹衝撞你
像一首詩受傷的支流

一滴水中　到處是死者
窗外　腐爛越逼真陽光越鮮豔
男孩子在摔倒的地方隱沒
軀體聽見　不認識的血大聲哭泣

在你裡面哭的愛　來自空中的肉色翅膀
沒有皮膚的河　整夜會疼痛
用你的一天覆蓋所有人的昨天
赤腳蹚過草地上的影子
花朵預約下一次手術
春天越泛濫越酷似一個無夢的人
什麼也不說時　沒有河能流出你

只有　黑暗骨髓裡你一直忍受的
都活著　啄　食

重新是一切

Spring, or a river's pain in your love

a bird's bright fear is in your gaze
a river's pain in your love

a shattered day   prevents you from dodging
this riverbed heaped high with snow-white ice
in a field of vision where notebooks thickly sprout
every tree beats against you
like a poem's wounded tributaries

in a drop of water   the dead are everywhere
outside the window   the brighter the sunlight the more lifelike the canker
a boy disappears where he falls
a body hears   unrecognised blood's loud wail

love weeping inside you   comes from flesh-coloured wings in air
a skinless river   hurts all night long
capping everyone's yesterdays with your one day
wading barefoot through shadows on the grass
flowers book operations to come
the more spring's in spate the more it's a lifelike dreamless man
when nothing's said   no river can flow away from you

there's only   what you've always endured in dark marrow
all alive   pecking   pecking

it's everything   all over again

夢，或每一條河的第三岸

綠色是最野蠻的匕首
而一個夢　犯罪般固守昨天的田野
固守在每棵杉樹的木頭椅子上
死者開學了

誰做夢　誰就得
跟隨一個春天流入這條河
跟著河　拍打白色骸骨間的第三岸

這片白色愛情既非存在又非幻象
卻把每天的玫瑰逼入險境
讓你在一場大火中回到過去
一支童年開始演奏的樂曲越聽越恐怖
被黑暗保鮮的傷口　像夜晚的房間
手壓在心上也有回聲
越來越空的　被河底包圍了
夢中才承認　厄運像詩人無法避開

這是你自己的厄運
整整一生是睜大眼睛的一夜
被你夢見的土地在你腳下不斷崩潰
陷進肉裡時　擁有沉淪的
深度　第三岸上沒人睡去或醒來

Dreams, or each river's third bank

green is the most brutal of bayonets
but a dream   fixes down yesterday's fields like a   crime
fixed in the pine tree's wooden chairs
the dead have started school again

who dreams   must
follow a springtime and flow into this river
follow the river   slap the third bank between white bones

this white love is neither existence nor fantasy
but forces each day's roses into the danger zone
through a great fire sends you back to your past
melodies first played in childhood more harrowing with each hearing
wound kept fresh by darkness   like a twilight room
a hand pressed on the heart will echo too
emptier and emptier   surrounded by the riverbed
only in dreams acknowledging   misfortunes a poet can't escape

this is your own misfortune
a whole life a long night with eyes open wide
the land you dreamed decays and decays under your feet
when it's sunk into flesh   it's deep
as damnation   on the third bank no one sleeps or wakes

安魂曲，或倒流的河

沒有一次愛情不是毀於愛情之中
像天空癱瘓在天空中
安魂曲　爲聾了的耳朵演奏就夠了

石頭的高音震顫中
每條河其實在倒流
從鳥叫聲倒流　樹比早晨更蒼白
從笑聲倒流　母親收藏的春天的盒子
準時被一個狂暴的孩子撕開

你還得返回你一直站立的地點

安魂曲　誰聆聽誰就是死者
誰唱　幽靈就穿上肉體　再次被遺棄
牙齒閃耀於淡黃色月光之外
記憶　在靜止中靜止
是音樂深處的天空

直到一切名字都說出死亡

而死亡用樂器說
放棄呼救的每條河　倒流成這無聲的
倒流進此刻　孩子爬上綠色長椅
木椿們又被大海的保姆拍著開花
春天　春天整齊列隊
你已死過　因此不怕去愛

Requiem, or river running back

no love not destroyed in love
like sky paralysed in sky
requiem   playing for deafened ears   enough

in the shimmering soprano of stones
each river really is running back
running back from birdsong   trees paler than morning
running back from laughter   the box of springtime mother collected
torn open in time by crazy children

you must still go back to where you have always stood

requiem   who listens with respect is the dead
someone sings   and spirit puts on flesh   abandoned again and again
teeth gleam beyond pale yellow moonlight
memory   standstill in standstill
is the sky of music's depth

until all names spell out death

and with musical instruments death says
rivers that give up crying for help   run back to become this silence
run back into this instant   children climb on green benches
wooden stakes slapped into flower again by nanny ocean
spring   spring is lined up trim and spruce
you've already died   so you're not afraid to love

黑暗們

一

綠葉總是被遺忘在　窗口太綠了的時候
像春天用力擲出的每一粒石子
都擊中春天自己

鳥兒　仍穿著藍色的旱冰鞋
老狗的眼睛卻厭倦了

河岸的拍打聲用不著翻譯
死亡的美學　唆使花朵們蜂擁而出

惟一忍住狂暴內心的　只有田野
逃得更遠時　四月嗅出了血液
陽光中樹林守在我們身後
那不能帶走的知識　又把死者帶走
朗誦一首詩　被加深的寂靜

另一個世界還是這個世界　黑暗說

二

沒有故事的人　用逃出日子的姿勢
逃進一個日子

沒有過去的人　過去了
海鷗被暮色製成一本抽象的書

鎖在隔離病房裡　誰不是瘋子
妄想　比肉體更像片斷

玻璃的片斷　骨骼碎裂聲響在外圍
舌根腐爛的片斷　黃昏為流失而流失

老鼠們叫著　光踩疼自己時的尖叫
每天被每天嚇醒了

同一個黑夜　沒有人的故事
再講一次仍不會發生　黑暗說

16

Darknesses

1

green leaves always forgotten when   windows are too green
like every pebble roughly thrown by spring
hitting spring itself

birds   still wearing arid skates of blue
though old dog eyes are tired out

no need to translate the riverbank's slapping
the aesthetics of death   incite the swarming of the flowers

fields alone   can tolerate the furious heart
fleeing still further   April sniffs out blood
in sunlight the wood crouches behind us
knowledge that can't be taken away   it takes away the dead
reciting a poem   a deepened stillness

the other world is still this world   darkness would say

2

a storyless person   escapes into a day
with a gesture of escaping from the day

a pastless person   has passed away
seagulls worked into an abstract book by the evening

locked in the isolation ward   who isn't crazy
delusions   more like fragments than flesh

fragments of glass   shattering skeleton heard on the periphery
fragments of rotting tongue   twilight washes away, just washes away

rats squeal   shrill squeals as light stamps on itself
each day startled awake by each day

with one black night   a personless story
still won't come true told twice   darkness would say

黑暗們

三

每一場雨都使你坐在自己的終點上
雨聲敲打屋頂　小動物的腳步
把你靜止地移入黑暗
在靜止的天氣裡你需要別人睡去
睡眠就是離開　雨季的整個世界離開
黑暗才穿過你像一匹烈馬穿過火焰
在你裡面聽　四周銀白的針腳
縫補一件肉質的破舊風衣

每一場雨只落進這片空地
你從終點讀起時　一頁黑色的說明
不疲倦地爲下個白晝更換一個人
篡改一個住址　墓地的街更泥濘
挑剔一隻手　乞丐們彼此仇恨地擁擠
組成無處躲雨的城市
大群濕漉漉的烏鴉在你裡面衝撞
繁殖長著共同面孔的不同罪惡　黑暗說

四

但黑暗什麼也沒說　黑暗與黑暗之間
僅僅是這個春天

風箏的骨頭掛在樹梢上
樹皮發亮　接吻的情人走過樹下
花粉在肺裡敲著去年的鑼
一個鮮紅的小丑　總能讓孩子狂奔

嚼著小手的牙越來越綠
舊報紙的草坪　交給火焰的剪子
四月　就以河流爲幻影
河流那忘卻的顏色　以我們爲幻影
鴿哨燒焦後　所有星星
被孩子玩夠了塞進一座漆黑的閘門

黑暗中總有一具軀體漂回不作夢的地點

3

each shower of rain makes you sit at your end
rain rapping on the roof   tiny animal steps
move you motionlessly into the darkness
in motionless weather you need others to sleep
to sleep is to leave   the world of the rainy season leaves
once darkness has passed through you like a thoroughbred through the fire
hear inside you   silvery white stitches everywhere
stitching a worn-out windcheater of flesh

every shower falls only on this bare ground
when you begin reading from your end   a page of black explanation
unweariedly swaps someone else for next day
forges an address   the graveyard street still muddier
finds fault with this hand   beggars huddle together in mutual hatred
making a city with nowhere to shelter from the rain
a flock of soaking crows collides inside you
breeds different crimes with identical faces   darkness would say

4

but darkness didn't say a thing   between dark and dark
only this spring

kite's bones hang in the treetops
bark shines   lovers pass kissing under the tree
pollen in the lungs beating last year's gong
a bright red clown   always makes children run wild

greener and greener the teeth that chew little hands
old newspaper lawn   hands over scissors of flame
so April   sees the river flow like a mirage
the current's forgotten colours   see us as mirages
once the dove's call is burned black   all the stars
are broken toys stuffed in a pitch-black floodgate

in darkness there's always a body drifting back to the place of no dreaming

連我們怕　也只怕自己的恐懼
黑暗什麼也不說　街頭每一個行人
就開始喃喃自語
黑暗　在聆聽嘴唇上塗抹的猩紅色黑暗

一座春天的學校永遠讓我們無知
一個記憶　誰活在其中誰就是鬼魂
而疾病使表情變薄
鏡子戴在臉上時　大海消化一尾死魚
被嘔吐著仍喋喋不休

黑暗太多了　以致生命從未抵達它一次
春天走出我們　春天才終於沉默

even we fear   only fear our own terror
darkness doesn't say a thing   every walker on the streets
starts muttering to himself
darkness   is listening to the orange-red darkness of lipstick

a spring school always makes us ignorant
memory   who lives in it is a ghost
but sickness attenuates the look
when a mirror's worn on the face   the ocean digests a dead fish
being vomited is still endless chatter

darknesses are too many   for life ever to have got there
spring walks out of us   only then   is spring silent at last

HOUSE LIKE SHADOW

類似陰影的房子

烏鴉的命題

烏鴉的語言裡每個早晨再死一次
烏鴉用黑暗　炫耀光
綠色的墓地就再次被踩實
森林顯出輪廓
死者的肉在松樹裡發胖
而耳朵又薄又透明　連夜掛滿枝頭
死後的寂靜　把你們驚醒

死了　才聽見一顆醜陋的腦袋
思想怎樣收割一場風暴
準時探進臥室哈哈大笑的腦袋
傲慢得像個禿了頂的獄卒
烏鴉　裹緊向黑夜租借來的制服
更赤裸

在夏季的書面上燙金
漫步草坪的稚嫩小手——拔光了指甲
你們的課本在夢中編印
在睡眠裡上學　渾身插滿羽毛地
游泳　聽見河水
鑿開軀體中比光線更白的洞穴

再次被那聽不見的　嚇得大聲啼叫

Crow's proposition

each morning dies once again in crow's language
crow uses darkness   to display light
green graves   trampled over and over
deep woods show off contours
flesh of the dead fattening in pine trees
yet thin and transparent ears   are hung from every branch at night
silence after death   wakes you all with a start

dead   only now hearing in the ugly brain
how thought harvests the storm
brain that punctually pokes into bedrooms to laugh
arrogant as a bald-headed jailer
crow   wrapped in the borrowed livery of the night
more naked still

gold on the letters of summer
little unfledged hands slow-marching on the grass
tear out fingernails one by one
your textbooks printed in dreams
schooled in sleep   swim
in a feathered skin   hear the river
bore in the body a cavern brighter than light

scared into loud cawing again   by what can't be heard

月食

一絲甜甜的血抹進你的嘴
你愛喝的劇毒的血
乳房裡的泥濘　藍色流淌的果醬

一隻最柔軟的手把你肉體的
紙　浸濕了水
你愛喝的不純的死亡

那掌聲　飼養多年的爬行動物
等在你被弄髒的一剎那
圍觀你的輕蔑

兩小時　女孩子們坐在草地上
互相撫摸　侵犯
背誦不純潔的詩

許多裙子裡　影子的鑰匙在開鎖
許多骨骼輻射出垂危的光
當整個天空響徹吞咽聲

你愛喝的夜　喝下你
一個被放棄的女人喝乾自己的奶
黑暗　躍入黑暗的游泳池

目睹子宮那隻黃白色的杯子
越涮洗越污穢
兩小時後　繼續謊言式的存在

Eclipse of the moon

a trickle of sweet blood drips into your mouth
toxic blood you love drinking
slushy in the tit   blue trickle of jam

the gentlest of hands has soaked the paper
of your flesh   with water
that impure death you love drinking

that clapping   for years fed crawling things
an instant that waits for you to be dirtied
surveys your scorn

two hours   girls sit on the grass
fondle each other   take liberties
memorise impure poems

in skirts   the keys of shadow are opening locks
light of skeletons emits terminally ill radiation
as all the sky echoes with sobs

night you love drinking   drinks you
a forsaken woman drinks her own milk dry
darkness   leaps into the dark pool

to witness the womb   that off-white glass
get filthier with each washing
two hours later   life's lying goes on

類似陰影的房子

那是你的房子　類似陰影的房子
在草地上擴大黃昏的建築
鳥聲被天空擊落　樹葉細小的舌頭
又議論著疲倦的風暴
影子也疲倦了　盲人們列隊
茫然摔下懸崖

那是你的房子　沒有你的房子
你被欠下像惡夢的債
一隻田鼠跳到地板上生病和打滑
類似陰影的田鼠
臉總是越來越黑的
類似玫瑰色的嘴　把挽歌的門咬開了
日子死去時你住進腐爛的燭火

當四壁模擬生活啞口無言
光　騎著最單薄的石頭潛入地下

潛入你　陰影類似一個主人
慷慨地敞開夜的陽台　眺望那風景
又一隻野貓追上自己的驚恐
又一顆頭顱　被釘進星群的釘子結束
類似荒草一片銀白
癱瘓的黑暗筆直聳立起來
塗掉一天衰老一歲的你
像可怕的月光　塗掉這片空地

House like shadow

that's your house   a house like shadow
a building on a lawn enlarges twilight
birdsong shot down by the sky   delicate tongues of leaves
discuss the exhausted storm again
shadows exhausted too   blind men line up
fall blankly over the precipice

that's your house   house with no you
you're owed like a debt of nightmares
a mouse jumps to the floor, sickens and slides
mouse like shadow
face always blacker and blacker
mouth the colour of roses   bites open the gate of elegy
as day dies you move into a rotting candle

as four walls are struck dumb imitating life
light   sneaks underground astride the frailest stone

sneaks into you   an owner like shadow
passionately opens night's balcony   views the scene
another wild cat chases its own fear
another skull   meets its end nailed to the stars
a weed-like silver-white
paralysed darkness towers up straight as a die
blots out the one-year-old you who will some day grow old
like terrible moonlight   blots out this vacant ground

方舟

你們總是沉沒於一片早已經過的水域
當森林不變的寂靜
磨利了斧頭
樹樁發黑的腳趾四處走動
松果的墜落聲　為夏天作出解釋
松針鋪滿一條火紅的道路
頭腦　是頭腦留下登陸的痕跡

是一塊岩石在火中爆裂
是看著大火的眼睛　終年感到寒冷
被記憶復活的白雪
是斧刃從兩行字之間向天空揮去
揮霍綠色　一棵樹酷似另一棵
揮舞睡眠　啄木鳥的洪水

把鼾聲狠狠拋出此刻
拋進　肉裡栽種的瘟疫
陳述往事的青草們　呲出地下的牙
喊叫　卻被木頭耳朵蓄意錯過
死寂牢房裡瘋子惟一的錯
是總會醒來　到昨天才醒來
過去的枝頭　目測著海底蒼白的磷火
用鳥兒背誦你們嘴裡霉爛的詩

Ark

you're always sunk in waters that passed by long ago
as the unchanging silence of the forest
has sharpened the axe
blackened toes of tree stumps walk all around
sound of falling pine kernels   explaining summer
pine needles cover a fiery red path
brain   it's only brain leaves embarcation scars

is a rock splitting in fire
is an eye watching a great fire   feeling cold all the year
white snow revived by memory
is an axeblade brandished at the sky from between the lines
squandering green   tree cruelly like another tree
wielding sleep   a flood of woodpeckers

mercilessly throw snoring out of this instant
throw it into   the plague planted in flesh
green grasses that declare the past   baring underground teeth
cry out   maliciously missed by wooden ears
in the cell's deathlike stillness the madman's only mistake
is to be always waking   only yesterday he woke
a branch of the past   sounding the seabed's pale phosphorescence
uses birds to recite the poems that moulder in your mouths

鄰居　　(一)

你們在相鄰的鍋裡烹調的死亡很鮮美
你們相鄰的壁爐裡
一節松木靜靜燃燒了百年

夏天總是陰冷的　像飼養長春藤的石牆
而道路穿過火深入冬天

從火中觀看　窗戶
仍一一刷洗慘白的夜
松樹被修剪的鐵皮影子站在窗外
刪改你們的骨骼

綠太陽無須敲門就闖進石頭
一個字闖進兩首詩的邪惡風景
證實　詩人脫臼的嘴
你們相似如一同烘烤的魚

鄰居　　(二)

　　　　　　另一個時間裡
天空沉重的藍　把鳥兒壓進一塊黏土
黃昏的光是樹幹上勤奮的鋸子
木樁淒慘微笑　一個無力的報復

　　　　　　隔離我們的時間
一張骸骨形狀的桌子緊挨另一張
不曾走開的死者
像燈　在松塔裡無聲爆炸
震動烏黑蝙蝠毛茸茸的耳膜

　　　　　　另一刻
我們還是這片寂靜未完成的作品
被各自的嗓音壓進黏土　剩下
作為一個辭的今日
作為著名的舌頭爬過古舊的瓷器

Neighbours I

a tasty death is cooking in your pot next door
in your neighbour's grate
a pine log quietly incinerates a hundred years

summer's always gloomy   like walls that succour ivy
yet the road goes through fire to winter's end

looking out from fire   windows
still wash the dim night clean one by one
the pines' clipped iron shadows stand outside the window
revising your skeletons

green sun bursts into stones without knocking
the vicious scene when one word bursts into two poems
affirms   the poet's dislocated mouth
you look like fish all barbecued together

Neighbours II

in another time
sky's heavy blue   rams birds into the clay
twilight a diligent saw on the branches
tree stump's tragic smile   a powerless revenge

in a time that separates us
a skeleton-shaped table squeezes up to another
the dead who never left
like lamps   silently explode in the pinecones
shake bats' downy jetblack ears

another moment
we are still this silent unfinished work
rammed into the clay by each voice   left
to be a one-word today
to be a famous tongue that once crawled on antique china

鄰居　（三）

被遺忘是一種幸運　她說
讓不知疲倦的人去學習記憶吧

每個女人始於觸摸自己的肉體
她說　一切黑暗智慧都與腐爛吻合

血　點燃最後一枝蠟燭
紫色的夜空就開始紡織傷口

一隻蛆蟲挖掘隧道藏起小小的死
落網的過冬的死

死者　也像一個沒人閱讀的作者
懷著隱秘的孩子在樓下走動

天使　乳房乾癟的蝙蝠
收攏翅膀倒掛在雪白皮膚下

她說　謀殺的手已經借累了
厭倦是僅有的床

小湖上水蛇出沒
她站在岸邊　是與自己無關的月光

月食時摸到肉裡滲出黑色沼澤
一個女人就那麼變成別的

鄰居　（四）

與死者最鄰近的是一首生者的詩
一座可能的墓穴隱匿在天上
像不可能的閣樓　緊鎖在塵土中
一隻蜘蛛或一隻蒼蠅
屍體都是鬼魂預約居住的雕花箱子
等待我的手　打開時留下指紋
樓梯的老鼠一踩就復活

Neighbours III

to be forgotten is good fortune   she says
let those who don't know weariness learn to remember

every woman begins by touching her body
she says   all dark wisdom coincides with corruption

blood   lights the last candle
then the purple night sky starts spinning wounds

a maggot digging a tunnel conceals a tiny death
trapped, hibernating death

a dead woman   like an unread author
walks about downstairs pregnant with a secret child

angels   bats with wizened paps   draw in their wings
hang upside down beneath snow-white skin

she says   the murderous hand is tired of being lent
boredom is the only bed

on the little lake the watersnakes come and go
she stands on the bank   is moonlight unconcerned with itself

when a lunar eclipse touches flesh a black swamp seeps out
so a woman changes into something else

Neighbours IV

closest to the dead is a poem by someone living
a possible grave hidden in the sky
like an impossible attic   locked in the dust
spider or fly corpses
carved boxes designed for ghostly living
until my hand   opens the chance-left fingerprints
mice on the stair stepped on and revived

吵醒百年前的光
吱吱叫著　割下詩人狂想的影子
一塊站在瓦上的雲
習慣腐爛出灰白色的踝骨
舉行一次與生者最鄰近的朗誦
像遺物們翻撿我的手指
出示了　每個人應得的恥辱

鄰居　（五）

我們的肉砌成窗台
我們從火中　觀看一節松木著火
某隻蜷縮的手腕
抽搐　顫抖　驟然伸出野獸的爪子

火與火鑄造一面鏡子
使潛入水銀深處的
都被目光刨出　我們站在自己窗外

被一把虛無的鑿子鑿出臉
鋒利的臉　雕刻花瓶中升起的舌頭
風聲在咽喉裡繁衍　招緊時
詩人　破舊胎衣般被一首詩脫落

土地的紅色鐵門總在耳邊匡匡關閉
墓碑　比我們更有名
肥沃屍首的宴席
一百年兩側暴露的眼睛都是攣生的

發狂的　什麼也沒寫下
才被死在心裡的刻出了

才自言自語　才怕冷
用野獸和火的爪子抓著牌　一張紙牌
隔開兩個彼此觀看的傷口　我們

light woken a century past
is squeaking   cuts down the poet's crazy shadow
cloud standing on the slates
in the habit of mouldering into a grey-white ankle
a single recitation closest to the living
that like relics casually checks my fingers
has shown   the shame we all should feel

Neighbours V

our flesh bricked up the windowsill
from the flame   we watch a pine log catch flame
a curled-up wrist
twitch   shiver   abruptly stretch out wild beast's claws

flame and flame forged in a mirror
let all that's sunk deep in mercury
be scraped out by sight   we stand outside our own windows

with a chisel of nothingness carve out a face
keenly-honed face   tongue rising in a carved vase
as the sound of the wind multiplies in the throat   is gripped in a vice
a poet   like used-up afterbirth   is shed by the poem

the earth's red iron gates are always clanging shut at our ear
tombstones   more famous than us
fat feast of corpses
the eyes revealed on either side of a century are twins

were crazy   wrote nothing down
were only then carved out by what died in our hearts

only then soliloquised   only then feared the cold
grabbed the cards with claws of flame and of wild beasts   a playing card
separates two wounds   watching each other   us

作曲家的塔

一

木橋的方向也是死魚們腐爛的方向
雨　被銀色湖面染得漆黑

石頭　已朽得讓根抓住
長春藤扎進肉裡的厭恨的根

吐出雨聲　夏天像一張發霉的皮子
鳥鳴墜入一隻耳朵的饑餓陷阱

聽覺　就成了黎明的缺口
所有葬在塔裡的同時響在音樂裡

一個瘋子的頭濕漉漉浮出
使天空不斷崩潰　狂怒地翻動昨夜

而昨夜再也不會過去　你
四周陰郁的窗戶只開向一個人的疼痛

二

惟一的戰爭僅僅在聲音與沉默之間
你聽見屍首推開棺材破土而出

末日終於抵達一封蒼白的信
推遲的時間　剛好夠遺忘

用一隻血紅鳥兒的全新口音朗誦
死者醒來就又一次輸給死亡

你輸給　一頁樂譜上的一生
像個拆除者　被啞巴緊咬的牙教誨著

寫　長著人臉的草全有冬天的流向
肉體看不見地返回

肉體　就在樂曲中逝去更遠了
當否定的光從一個音符移到另一個

The composer's tower

1

the wooden bridge's direction is the rotten direction of dead fish
rain   dyed black by a silver lake

stone   rotted to let roots clutch
loathing's root that ivy stabs in flesh

spit out the sound of rain   summer like a mouldy pelt
birdsong plunging into the starving trap of the ear

hearing   turned into a breach in the dawn
everything interred in the tower sounds out in music

a madman's sodden head floats to the surface
makes the sky fall apart again and again   frenziedly stirs last night

but last night will never again pass by   you
dim windows all around opening only on one person's pain

2

the battle is only between sound and silence
you hear the corpse opening the lid and struggling up through the soil

the final day has arrived in the end at a pallid letter
time retarded just enough to forget

declaiming in the novel accents of a blood-red bird
the dead are wakened and lose to death again

you lose   to a life on a page of the score
like a wrecker   lectured by the clenched teeth of the dumb

write   every man-faced grass follows winter's flow
flesh invisibly returns

flesh   has elapsed in composition   gone further still now
as negating light moves from note to note

三

門砰地關上　　審問者的憤怒在變形
父親小聲申辯　　幾乎不像父親

塔裡有一隻十一歲的耳朵
卻以全部年齡貼著牆

繼續偷聽　　聲音怎樣死在聲音裡
像沉默　　創造一塊堆砌沉默的卵石

孩子站在高高的塔尖上
吞下黑暗星星塞進小手的邪惡

那風暴塞滿一隻寂靜的胃
六月這個早晨　　把你留進瘋子的昨夜

寫出最後一聲口哨
皮膚蒼老的塔　　這麼容易地被吹走

3

the door bangs shut   and the inquisitor's rage changes
a father softly explains himself   not at all like a father

there's an ear aged eleven in the tower
glued to the wall by all of its years

overhearing all the time   how sound dies in sound
like silence   creates a stone of heaped silence

a child stands on top of the high tower
swallows the evil dark stars stuff in his little hand

the storm stuffs a silent stomach full
this June morning   pulling you back into the madman's last night

writing out the final whistle
a tower of ageing skin   so easily blown away

陰郁的夏季

綠　無力滲入病人的皮膚更深時
夏季必然是陰郁的

每一滴雨已落下過五次
屋頂上沉重的沼澤蠕動了十次
田野　一床無處晾晒的褥子
在你思想裡排水
松針精雕細刻的耐心使光走向反面
死人腦怒因為找不到泥土的縫隙

陰郁的夏季裡　你甚至無力
構思最後一場風暴

摔碎種子以及種子裡的玻璃大樹
摔碎鳥蛋以及內臟保存的一聲慘叫
但辭摔不碎　每個辭是一把
盛滿血肉的木頭勺子
一百次從胎兒軀體中挖出被弄錯的天空

就對了　這夏季只是你的夏季
紅色站台上不朽的只是一種解釋
生銹的列車無須到達
你被死者呼出的空氣圍困一千次
肺　就是一條鮮艷的河
不流　肉做的墓碑上沒有缺口
每一個故事結束過兩千次

你盯著哪兒　那裡又開始哭泣

Dismal summer

when green   lacks strength to soak deeper into the patient's skin
summer is inevitably dismal

each drop of rain has already fallen five times
the heavy rooftop swamp rippled and heaved ten times
fields   a mattress with nowhere to hang out to dry
draining in your thoughts
the pine needle's carved patience infinitely reverses light
dead man raging because he can't find cracks in the mud

in the dismal summer   you're debilitated enough
to invent a final storm

shatter seeds and glass tree in the seed
shatter eggs and the cry of pain preserved in the viscera
but words can't be shattered   every word
a wooden hook of flesh and blood
a mistaken sky dug out from a foetus a hundred times

that's right   this summer is your summer
on the red platform what's immortal is only one explanation
the rusty train doesn't have to arrive
you're besieged by air breathed out by the dead a thousand times
lungs   a brightly-coloured river
unflowing   no loopholes in the headstone built by flesh
each story ended two thousand times

where you're staring   there   tears again

窗台上的石頭

窗台上的石頭望著窗外
它使整個房間向懸崖傾斜
活在沉船中的魚　都準備爛成魚刺
琴聲被一把斧頭砍伐
大樹仍在做一次綠色的五指練習
每場靜止於窗台上的暴風雨
都以靜止的方式打入屋內
像石頭冷漠的光芒打入你
整個大海向起點傾斜
你被監視著爬進一條軟體動物
無意中形同屍首
隨時可能被烏鴉啄起
玻璃放大了什麼也不說的威脅
一隻灰眼珠直瞪著你的臉　忽略你

Stone on the windowsill

stone on the windowsill looks out of the window
makes a whole room tilt to the cliff
fish living in sunken ships   ready to rot to bones
music hacked by the axe
trees still doing a green five-finger exercise
the rainstorm that always stands still at the window
uses its standstill to insinuate itself into the room
insinuates itself into you like the indifferent gleam of the stone
an entire ocean tilts to its beginning
as you are monitored you climb into an invertebrate
unwittingly shaped like a corpse
could be pecked by a crow anytime
the glass magnifies the threat without speaking
a grey eyeball staring at your face   ignoring you

怕冷的肖像

寒冷是不分季節的　像你背後的牆
松樹總在寓意一個下雪的日子
壁爐中的火焰也能綠得發黑
當火成爲一種現實　冷就躲不開
你怕　於是更像
那個一直被誤認爲你的人

別人　讓你定居時使你散發出藥味
被天空支配的圍巾裡全是雨夜
肖像們出門　你卻懸掛在
牆上　死後才學會怕一張被畫成的臉

陽光也被誤認了　它僅僅像光
手指在不動的風中像手指微微抽搐
一面鏡子也像瘋子
眼白痴呆　從未記住死魚們的大海
像冬天　把一口濃痰吐進你眼裡

凍結進軀體時　微笑是疲憊的裙子
謊言　只要溫暖就再說一遍
讓你更刺骨　酷似那肖像
寒冷是一個比喻　怕冷是另一個
一百年的鳥在別處叫起來
比喻一隻從死人頭上凍掉的棕色耳朵
像你自己的那麼可怕
那麼聾　那麼易於被辨認　被畫出

Portrait afraid of the cold

cold comes in any season   like the wall behind you
pine trees always imply a day of snow
flame in the hearth can turn so green it blackens
as fire becomes a reality   cold can't hide away
you fear   so more resemble
the one who is always mistaken for you

when someone else   settles you down you smell of medicine
in the scarf the sky controls there's only rainy night
portraits go through the door   but you hang
on the wall   you only learned to fear a painted face   after your death

sunlight mistaken too   only resembling light
fingers in the unmoving wind like fingers slightly twitching
a mirror is like a madman too
a white-eyed idiocy   an ocean that never remembered dead fish
like winter   gobbing thick in your eye

when the body's frozen   a smile is a weary skirt
lies   only spoken again if they warm you
chill you more to the bone   cruelly like this portrait
cold is a metaphor   fear of cold another
century-old bird crying elsewhere
image of a brown ear frozen off a corpse's head
terrible as your own
deaf enough to be   identified   or painted

森林中的暴力

糾纏的被扭斷的脖子上　天空豎起翻領
口號還在冒煙　天空已開始吃肉
樹林低下頭　而天空遠遠地笑
木樁堆著　天空忘記了

這是你每天看見的暴力

群居的綠色的腳
一陣死寂又一陣死寂地走向死後
聽到天空　滿意地在背後填土

雷雨　把你變成一塊濕漉漉的案板
刀剁在腰上多麼悅耳
陽光的唱針划破年輪　不再刺耳
樹身　努力接近了廢棄的事實

這是每天的暴力

天空　砍伐森林因為它正變成人
因為人每天不流血
像你欣賞著　寧靜中自己不停的抽搐

這是每天

Violence in the forest

tangled on broken necks   sky turns its collar up
slogans still smoking   sky has begun eating meat
woods bend their heads   and sky laughs far away
tree stumps piling up   sky has forgotten

this is the violence you see every day

gregarious green feet
running to death in a more and more deathly silence
hear sky   contentedly fill in earth behind them

thunderstorm   turns you to a soaking wet chopping board
how sweet to the ear a knife hacking at the back
sunlight's stylus scratches the growth-rings   they'll never grate again
tree trunks   have come with an effort to the truth of their disposal

this is everyday violence

sky   fells the forest because it's turning human
because people don't bleed every day
just as you enjoy   in peace and quiet   your endless twitching

this is every day

肖像的生活

這監獄仿造你們寂靜的肉體
一部傳記中被漏掉的次要角色
活著　僅僅爲服刑

爲了在每天分配的小小懸崖上
把砍下的頭重新擺好
溜出黃昏畫框的頭

都是咬斷過舌尖的
像家庭一樣　在雨中發黑
嵌進水泥翅膀的樹葉一片片發綠

那踩到老鼠或蛇身上的尖叫
準是紅的　讓午夜準時踩中你們
宣布延長空白的表情

沒人從死後回來摘掉自己
也沒人　敢看著自己
穿過盥洗室走進下個難忍的早晨

A portrait's life

this prison copies of all your silent bodies
the minor roles missed out of a biography
living   just to serve their sentence

to set out the severed heads again
on the little cliff that's distributed each day
heads that slip out of twilight's frame

all with tongues bitten off
like a family   blackening in the rain
leaves inlaid in concrete wings greening one by one

the shrill cry of stepped-on mice or snakes
is surely red   lets midnight step punctually into you
declares the lengthening of the blank white look

no one comes back after death to strip himself away
and no one   dares watch himself
cross the bathroom and walk into another unbearable morning

監獄島

光用一根根直立的柱子　建築它的廟宇
光在褐色的岩石上刻字　在海邊讀書
五月是一張旅館的床
早晨騎上　黑暗中被弄醒的
又藍又亮黏著夢的肉體
一片海的寬大葉子頂在酒杯頭上
一個日子把你關進一粒活水晶

　　你從未到達的島嶼
　　也從未離開過

漆黑的風暴是一隻大帆船
囚徒們還在浪聲中哭訴　　想家
想像一張犁從身上拉過
想像一些肉體　像鳥兒沒有肉體
喝乾你時讓你漲潮
一生看守著你的大海精疲力竭

　　狠狠打入你體內

一匹五月的白馬打入醉態
圍繞你奔跑　敞開綠色起伏的皮膚
眺望監獄島的眼睛自己是監獄
光　在海底折磨一條隧道
小小的空心的島　在體內脹著你
疼　就是一盞不滅的燈
再疼　海從早晨背後射出來
又一個白晝深深射入令你致命的方向

　　結束是冗長的
　　結束本身就沒有結束

52

Prison island

light builds its temple   with erect pillars one by one
light carves words on the dull brown stone   reads by the sea
May is a hotel bed
morning rides   a bright blue body glued with dreams
that was woken in the dark
a sea's broad leaf balances on a wineglass
a day ushers you into a grain of living crystal

the islands you never reached
you never left either

the pitch black storm is a sailing ship
prisoners still tearfully complain in the surf   homesick
imagine a plough pulled from their bodies
imagine bodies   as birds have no bodies
when you are drunk dry you are at flood tide
keeping watch all your life on the exhaustion of your ocean

pitilessly banished to your body

the white horse of May is banished to drunkenness
galloping all around you   opening the green rise and fall of the skin
eyes that look out over prison islands are prisons themselves
light   torments a tunnel on the seabed
tiny hollow islands   bloat you from inside
pain   is an unextinguished lamp
more pain   the sea shoots out from behind the morning
another day shoots deep in a fatal direction

ending is long and wearisome
ending itself has no end

傳記

一　讀到的

松樹還像長在中國墓地裡那樣呼吸
風卻靜靜改變白晝的方向
犁　反覆走到田野盡頭
綠色　一本八月的肥沃的書
生命播下死者的種子

夜晚　全部星星旅行在玉石的井底

整整一個夏天你讀一本傳記
松樹的影子浸著水
盛滿水的椅子刻成粗淺的浮雕
海仍在遠處孤零零激怒
鳥叫聲泛濫於天空　幾乎像不叫
你讀著彷彿什麼也沒讀

只有　搖盪一個下午使它變黑的藝術

二　被讀到的

彬彬有禮地懷著輕蔑
你詛咒一片風景時成為那兒一隻天鵝
往事不間斷的流水中　你的驚恐
依然像壞天氣輕易把你擊敗

依然是靜止的時間
墓地幽暗角落裡一塊石板
攤開最後一張被鞋跟踩出顴骨的臉

雨中一輛紅色公共汽車開到終點
一首詩　每天一次寫到終點
已不是你而只是你的瘋狂
沒有手　僅有一把為鏡子預訂的雨傘
目睹詩人被打字機修改著走近表情
近得被傳記脫掉短褲
向別人三小時的拷問交出一生

Biography

I *What's read*

pine trees breathe like they grow in a Chinese graveyard
but the wind calmly changes the direction of day
plough   goes back and forth to the field's end
green   a fertile August book
life scattering seeds of the dead

night   stars moving in a jade well

all of one summer you read a biography
pine tree shadows immersed in the water
chair full of water cut in shallow relief
far away sea still raging alone
birdsong floods the sky   as if there's no song
you read as if you've read nothing

there's only   art that sways and blackens an afternoon

II *What's being read*

when with polite contempt
you curse the scenery   you become a swan there
the water of the past flows incessantly   your panic
easily overcomes you still, like bad weather

it's still the time of stasis
a stone slab in a dim corner of the graveyard
spreads the last face whose cheekbone is stamped by a boot heel

in the rain a red bus drives to its destination
a poem   written each day to its destination
isn't you but your madness
no hands   only an umbrella ordered by the mirror
witnessing a typewriter-revised poet enter into expression
so close that underwear is taken off by biography
a life surrendered to three hours of someone else's torture

三　沒被讀到的

被夢見有時比作夢更危險
蠕動在皮膚下的是一滴血而非一個字
再也嗅不到昨天的傷口
那製作紅色蝴蝶標本的眩目怪癖
黃昏一個一個把你填入空格
小鐵床四面八方在臥室中尖叫奔走
你被你的惡夢運走
像電線盡頭　一滴
不會哭泣的玻璃眼淚

另一個夏季的讀者比你更陰郁
猶如你的作者
親吻你　你的舌尖腐爛了返青了
驚嚇你　你是不能報復的　無家的
昨天的病人被一本書銀白的鋸齒鋸著
被一個鑄鐵的名字逐出自己
因為天空已翻過了這一頁

四　沒讀的

螞蟻懂得怎樣爬過照片上的臉
螞蟻　在睜大的眼睛上行走
踩著黑色或肉色的辭

平坦　連閉緊也不敢
蟻酸使一個下午變黃　散開

一頭死貓的內臟聚集了蒼蠅
掛在窗外松樹間的鳥類大聲啼叫

誰也沒在讀　誰都
聽見一隻風暴的筆尖在紙上沙沙逼近
越過你　和你臉上的季節
眼珠　就像積雪在眼眶中坍塌
數著螞蟻輪流落下的腳

整個落入　死亡完美的想像

III *What hasn't been read*

to be dreamed is sometimes more dangerous than dreaming
what squirms beneath the skin is a drop of blood, not a word
yesterday's wounds can't smell any more
that glaring eccentricity that creates red specimen butterflies
one by one twilights use you to fill blank space
little iron bed rushing around the bedroom with shrill cries
you are transported by your nightmare
like the end of an electric wire   one
glass tear that cannot weep

readers in another summer are gloomier than you
just the way your writers
kiss you   your tongue rots and turns green
startle you   you have no revenge   no home
yesterday's patient sawn by the silver teeth of a book
driven from yourself by a cast-iron name
because the sky has turned this page over

IV *What's unread*

ants know how to climb the face in the photograph
ants   walk on wide-open eyes
treading on black or flesh-coloured words

smooth   wouldn't even dare shut tight
formic acid turns the afternoon yellow   diffuses

dead cat's innards gather flies
hanging from pine trees outside the window birds loudly cry

whoever isn't reading   hears
the penpoint of a storm rustling close on the paper
across you   and the seasons on your face
eyeballs   like snow crumbling in an eye socket
counting the ants' falling feet one by one

all falling into   death's perfect imagination

五　空白和插曲

晴朗的日子總是從大海開始
從一連串空白開始　從謊言開始

我們總是記錯時間　等待
修剪一座死去的花園摘到玫瑰
陽光下　紅白兩色的腦子在瘋長
追趕日記中煩亂的筆跡

我們記錯了　每天海風的鹹味
都是沒有地址的軀體
靜止不動的藍　被回憶編輯後才耀眼

被銷毀　灰燼的一生才繼續
修剪玫瑰直到花園被移栽在海面
充斥一個無人活過的時刻
以象形的敏感和象形的冷漠

六　沒讀卻讀到的

只有死亡流傳下去　在語言中落雪
只有嘴流傳下去哭喊母親
當天空無助得像一個呼吸的賽程
你被一隻蟬變得刺耳
八月　綠色中充滿腫脹的死者

只有孤獨　能給玻璃刻花
所有人被塞進一具肉體時加倍孤獨
使你沒有年齡去衰老
睡在忘卻裡的詩也睡在影子上

只有漂走　使你們彼此在自己身上
寫下別人　在夏天
一個死者年年落入松樹上的綠色大雪
黑夜的沙子就又漏下許多次
每次一個黎明　重讀被剔淨的經歷

V *Blank & interlude*

sunny days always start from the sea
start from continuous white   start from lies

we always misremember time   until
pruning a dead garden we pick roses
in sunlight   red brains and white all overgrown
chasing the disorderly handwriting in a diary

we misremembered   the salty smells of the sea-wind every day
being bodies without an address
static motionless blue   dazzles only after memory's editing

once incinerated   the life of ashes goes on
prune roses till the garden is transplanted to the sea
flood a moment no one has lived
with hieroglyphic sensitivity and hieroglyphic indifference

VI *What's read but unread*

only death hands down   snow falling in language
only a mouth is handed down to a wailing mother
as the sky is helpless as a breathing contest
you are made discordant by a cicada
August   green filled with the swollen dead

only loneliness   can engrave glass
loneliness doubles when everyone is squeezed into one body
making you grow old without an age
a poem that sleeps in forgetting also sleeps on shadows

only drifting   makes each of you write someone else
in your own life   each year in summer
a dead man falls into the green snow on the pine trees
sands of black night dripping again
each drip a daybreak   repeating experience picked clean

THE SKY SHIFTS

天空移動

走在牆上的斷腳

是否每堵牆繼續長高都能俯瞰海面
讓你學會不知恥辱地走
腳斷了才是一張驚恐的臉
看著軀體被踝骨丟棄
懸崖下的粉碎聲猶如你的鼾聲

暴風雨也發出木頭的腳步聲
所有窗戶敞開時　是一個封死的天空
像葉子的每個去年都掛在樹上
鋸倒的樹四季懷孕
鳥群被剔淨了　飛翔在終點之後

是否斷腳的哭泣聲就是無聲
趾甲一片慘白　才插進這片海的玻璃
想像一次不流血的越獄
你癱瘓在牆上　走
走著的春天卻砌進牆壁

萎縮成石頭　裸露下個沒學過的字
你得為一雙斷腳的笑聲簽字
那陣連鼾聲也沒切斷它的笑聲
海俯瞰你像個可怕的成績
早已在你臉上踩滿了污臭的腳印

Broken foot that walks the wall

whether or not every wall that grows higher can overlook the sea
will teach you to walk without shame
a broken foot is only a panicking face
watching a body abandoned by an anklebone
below the cliff a shattering sound so like your snore

a rainstorm makes the sound of wooden footsteps too
when every window is opening   it's a sky sealed tight
as on the trees hangs each last year of the leaves
sawn-down trees pregnant every season
flocks of birds scraped clean   hover behind the terminus

whether or not the weeping of a broken foot is silence
once toenails are ghostly pale   they dip into the glass of this sea
imagine a jailbreak that never once bleeds
you're paralysed on the wall   can't walk
but the walking spring is bricked into a wall

withering into stone   the next naked unlearned word
you must sign for the laughter of two broken feet
that laughter that even snoring hasn't shut off
the sea overlooks you as if a terrible success
has trampled foul footprints over your face

死羊羔的海

你們肉做的棺材早被釘死了
濕漉漉的羊毛下　海的肉
翻開一冊羶腥的書
讓裹著皮革睡在火旁的赤裸女人讀
大雪吞吃一群羊羔時是聾子
哀號嗆進鮮紅的肺
魚類死於破碎玻璃下徹底的白
羊眼　終於空虛得認出這片冬天的海
血液結冰　認出被擰斷的脖子
誰盯著風暴漸漸透明了

於是一切痛苦都是凍傷
小貓似的被抽掉骨骼的軀體
軟得又被雪咬下牙印
當你們的頭和著泥　成堆扔下卡車
恐懼　被趕進凍土深處擁擠取暖
灰黑的海水像一滴死後仍在啜飲的奶

春天出賣了你　它已遠遠逃離
夏天的精液一直在流汗
胎兒們卻從子宮的果凍裡探出鼻子
嗅著四隻奔向嚴寒的蹄子
奔進雪　夭折的器官終於發育成無痛的
死亡的鮮肉繁殖大片陰影
成千條牧羊犬撲入一扇窗戶狂吠
從海上看到你　報復性地停留在冬天

Sea of dead lambs

your fleshy coffin long since nailed shut
below soaking lambswool   sea's flesh
opens a rank book
makes a naked woman wrapped in hides read it by the fire
when snow swallows a flock of lambs it's deaf
wailing choked in a scarlet lung
fish die in utter whiteness below the shattered glass
sheep's eyes   finally empty enough to recognise this winter sea
blood freezes   recognises the wrung necks
someone turns slowly transparent staring into the storm

then all pain is frostbite
a catlike body, bones removed
so soft the biting snow leaves toothmarks
as your heads all balled with mud   abandon the truck in a pile
terror   driven deep into frozen ground   squeezes heat out
grey black seawater like a drop of milk suckled after death

spring has sold you out   it's long gone now
summer's semen was in sweat all along
but embryos poke from the womb's jelly
smell four hooves that rush towards the bitter chill
rush into snow   organs prematurely dead grow pain-free at last
death's bright flesh breeds vast shadows
sheepdogs by the thousand swoop in the window   madly barking
watching you from the sea   your revenge staying on through winter

刻有不同海洋名稱的博物館窗戶

沒有一片海洋像這片絕對靜止
字　癱瘓在窗戶上
被你讀到的不同風暴
深深刻入白色石壁
博物館唯一收藏的時間脆弱得像玻璃
你站在這兒　從海到海航行了多年
你看　樹木就再次被天空淹死
綠　寂靜威脅
讓一個海的名稱率領它的全部死者
沒人能抵達一片沒有名稱的海
讓一塊頭蓋骨活著暴露給春天的思想
墓碑的陳述絕對明亮

站在不同的海邊你被剝光了
海四面奔去　食肉的肥厚葉子們
是一張張卡片　鯊魚在標本中洄游
刻划活人遍佈水下的慘白牙齒
水滴絕對飢渴
被徹底剝奪時　一架空想的鋼琴被砸碎
一種看見透明得以眼睛為結束
玻璃的說謊聲　僅僅使耳朵更刺耳
你摸到的只有自己指紋間的波浪
被相同的瘋狂扼死在窗戶另一側

月亮的淡黃色頭蓋骨　讓歲月磨刀
月光在博物館臉上雕刻早被它毀滅的
所有海洋的沉重樹冠
用你扎根　讓春天湧入就是湧出
死亡像一顆比你更綠的種子
不變的時間裡　海面上的足跡一直在絞痛
不知是誰的名稱使葬禮不得不無限
一扇永遠關閉的窗戶
把大海盛在瓶子外面　惟一溢出了光
那風暴死去後凝聚到你身上的磷光
絕對　熄滅在你返回之前

Museum windows carved with the names of different oceans

no ocean like this absolute standstill
words   paralysed on windows
a different storm which you read
carved deep in the stone wall
the only time the museum collects is fragile as the glass
you stand here   have sailed many years from sea to sea
you see   trees drowned again by the sky
green   silent menace
let a sea's name command all its dead
no one can reach an unnamed sea
let a living skull lay bare its thought to the spring
the tombstone's statement shines absolutely clear

standing by a different shore you have been stripped bare
the sea rushes all around   all plump carnivorous leaves
are cards   sharks migrate among the specimens
pale teeth that scratch living souls are everywhere underwater
water-drops have absolute hunger and thirst
when utterly deprived   a fantasy piano is shattered
that watching so transparent   its ending is an eye
the lying voice of glass   only makes an ear more piercing
what you touch is simply the waves of your own fingerprints
throttled by the same madness on another side of the window

the moon's pale yellow skull   makes time sharpen its knife
on the museum's face moonlight carves what it long since destroyed
the heavy canopies of every ocean
using you to take root   to let spring pour in is a pouring out
death like a seed much greener than you
in unchanging time   footprints on the sea have all along been in pain
unknown what name forced the funeral to be infinite
a window forever shut
holds the ocean outside a bottle   all that spills is light
the storm condenses after death into phosphorescence on your body
absolutely   extinguished before you come back

天空移動

你知道那裡什麼也沒有　連天空也沒有
雪白的屍骨被大片藍色解散時
一塊墓地的甲板總看得頭暈目眩
每個黎明急劇萎縮
窗口　就像一座講台被刺眼的光照亮
風暴演講聲裡你那張小床
仍在退入昨夜沒有你的方向
沒有鳥　水泥的雲成群從樹上轟起
你越瘋狂地抬頭嘴裡越湧滿血腥

移動的是這張地圖　離開你痛哭的位置
磨損的鞋底放肆地用你眼睛擦腳
移動的是隻藍色的豹　牛羊們哀鳴中
一千次被屠宰的老人呼喊母親
你得坐進這個像隧道的地點
聆聽死亡不得不移動時　被移動

被一顆星星的方向留在相反的方向
被你睡眠中也在失去的　整理成辭句
月亮每天為被領走的肉體發黃
像口床單上的痰

腐爛　就不分性別地移入白色封面
讓天空在你裡面翻閱你
父親站滿視野　代代傳授這孤獨
鳥群急躁地互相穿透　狂奔向你自己
雪盲症患者臉上貓頭鷹的笑容
那就是過去　天空移動的破敗門廊裡
你不看也已過去　又明亮又空曠
壓迫一顆樹突起漆黑的前景

The sky shifts

you know there's nothing there   not even the sky
when a snow-white skeleton is dissolved by a sheet of blue
the grave's deck always watches till it's dizzy
every daybreak rapidly withers
window   like a rostrum lit by dazzling beams
your little bed in the sound of the storm's lecture
still retreats into last night   that direction where there was no you
there are no birds   flocks of cement clouds boom in the trees
the more you madly lift your head the more gushing blood fills your mouth

what's shifted is this map   leaving the place of your bitter tears
down at heel shoes presumptuously wipe their feet on your eyes
what's shifted is a blue panther   in the wailing of cows and sheep
the old man butchered a thousand times cries for his mother
you must sit down into this tunnel-like place
when listening with respect to death makes you shift   be shifted

be by a star's direction left facing the opposite direction
be what's lost in your sleep too   edited into words
every day moonlight turns yellow for flesh made to flee
like phlegm on the sheets

corruption shifts into the white book jacket unconcerned by sex
makes the sky inside you browse you through
father standing fills your vision
a loneliness handed down from generation to generation
herds of horses rashly intermingle   run wild at you
an owlish smile on the face of the snow-blind
that's the past   in the ruined porch of the shifting sky
you are past and see nothing   void and bright
forcing a single tree to tower above a pitch black foreground

世界的軀體

沒有一顆牙齒會死亡　你的或鱷魚的
只要這木雕依然端坐
在門口　揮霍做夢的古老能力
夢見早晨是條幽暗的走廊
許多張嘴　探出胸前一起吃肉
許多風吹動草編的巨大耳環
鯊魚懷著險惡的念頭從背後爬樹
爬上一張海洋的凳子

沒有　妄想之外多餘的部分
只要被剷去生殖器的白內障貝殼們
還陷進不會抽搐的眼眶

沉船響到海底的汽笛聲　就像門鈴聲
客人行走中已被珊瑚剔淨
粉紅色骨頭上　書信當然是色情的
生日鏡子裡女孩被逼進牆角
再次　乞求
你無血的軀體壓在睡熟了的小小鬼魂上

不停拉鋸
不朽　一顆無夢的腦袋更像夢
臉的黑暗想像　把臉在腳下撐緊
假　才存在了
燈光照耀下才不變

你胃裡兩個酸臭飽嗝間遠離上千歲

坐著　大海和樹木就綠了
鑿刻　故事裡的天空一份白色早餐
讓你逃不出每天的飢餓
也抵達不了　這可怕地址上
一個摸到自己是食肉魚類的人
穿過走廊　五官在一朵木頭玫瑰裡乾裂
活　被夢見

Body of the world

no tooth that can die   yours or the crocodile's
if this wood carving will only sit up straight
at the door   squander the ancient power of dreaming
dream morning is a dark corridor
open mouths   poking from chests to eat meat
winds blow huge ear-rings of straw
sharks with sinister intent climb trees behind your back
climb on the bench of the ocean

no   the excess beyond delirium
if only white cataract shells with gouged-out genitals
still sink into an eye-socket that cannot twitch

ship's sirens that sound on the seabed   are like doorbells
the stranger in his travels has been scraped clean by coral
on pink bones   letters are of course sexy
the girl in the birthday mirror forced into a corner
begging   over and over
your bloodless flesh pressing on a tiny soul familiar from deep sleep

non-stop sawing
eternity   an undreaming brain more like a dream
a face's dark imagination   wrings the brain out underfoot
falsity   has only existed
only unchanging under lamplight

between sour belches your stomach is thousands of years away

sitting   ocean and trees green now
chisel   the sky in the story's white breakfast
makes you unable to escape a daily hunger
and unable to reach   this terrible address
like a flesh-eating fish you touch yourself
having come through the corridor   sense-organs split in a wooden rose
living   being dreamed

所有不在的房子

死鴿子的翅膀組成黑夜
腋下鮮紅的肉　懷孕的女人在嘔吐
死鴿子是隻從陽台上跌落的球
所有不在的都肥胖
腥臭　像死鴿子弄髒牆壁的叫聲

在你身上死去的房子
自己就是一場瘋狂的睡眠

所有被夢見的只是一個人的鬼魂
所有停在你生前的大雪
把男孩子照料成樹木的陰影
走投無路的血液　依舊複寫出春天
花朵　更加麻木地複寫在紙上
你被迫駒在每個死鴿子築巢的地址上

聽著門窗被釘死
在你深處　鄰居們近親繁殖
依然用一口昨天吐出的墨綠膽汁洗澡
樓梯陷落時　天空中響起舞步

所有最悲慘的移動仍是一間房子的移動

移入這不在的　白色言辭
有的是時間讓死鴿子孵出它的鳥蛋
你有的是時間從一張床到另一張
睡過一個黑夜就留下一具屍體
一對肉質翅膀　剛觸及水下的月亮
有的是時間住進
淘汰大海的光芒　被過去時終於被指出

All the rooms that aren't there

dead dove's wings form the dark night
scarlet flesh in the armpit   pregnant woman vomiting
dead dove is a ball that tumbles from the balcony
all that's not there is gross
rank   like the cry of a dead dove that dirties the walls

rooms that die in you
are themselves a crazy sleep

all that's dreamed is only one person's soul
all the snow that stops in your lifetime
turns a boy into a tree's shadow with its caring
cornered blood   as always duplicates spring
flowers   still more numbly duplicate on the paper
you are forced to lie in every address where dead doves hatch

hearing doors and windows nailed shut
deep inside you   neighbours all inbred
still wash with inky bile they threw up yesterday
when a staircase founders   dance steps sound in the sky

all the most miserable shifting is still the shifting of a house

move into this that's not there   what white words
have is time to make a dead dove hatch its eggs
what you have is time from one bed to another
to oversleep one dark night and leave a corpse behind
a pair of fleshy wings   has just touched the moon under the water
has time to move in
the radiance that eliminates the ocean   is finally pointed out when it's past

時間海岸　（一）

狂風已把樹吹到邊緣　累了的岩石
仍繼續向下滾動

一隻昨夜死去的鳥留下驚叫
那女性的尖叫　在陽光中反芻

一個人被海命令時
不得不再次赤裸
於是任何一張床都擺在海邊
任何一條魚都占用你們的腹部散發腥味
魚眼　聚集了被看見的白
那天空的刺眼的白　讓你用十月做夢
讓你在夢中提醒自己夢不是真的
當雲急急移動　代替你的移動
漲潮　為每天澆鑄一塊混凝土地面
死後的划槳聲
這片松針的綠抬起你狠狠卸下你

是一張從斑馬臉上剝下的皮製成田野
是鐘表的肉　使你不能行走
你站著　海狗們就像陰影圍攏狂吠
一雙看著時間的眼睛看到被釘死的窗戶
是你　把大海變老了

盡頭　太單調的藍找不到一個字
語言終止於你的語言　島仍像癱瘓的背
十月終止於你怕冷的一剎那
裸體浴場摩擦著一塊被放大的屍斑
海在死亡中無限逼近時更像一個界限
是自己暴露在自己盡頭　是盡頭
讓一百年鮮豔得像一隻有毒的孔雀
因為沒有　才吞沒你

The shore of time   1

crazy gale has blown trees to the limit   weary stones
                    still keep rolling down

a bird that died last night leaves behind a scream
that shrill female cry   ruminates in the sunlight

a person commanded by the sea
can't help being naked again and again
so any bed is set by the shore
any fish employs your bellies to emit a rank stench
fish eyes   have gathered the white that is seen
that sky's ear-piercing white   makes you dream with October
reminds you in your dream that dreams are unreal
as clouds busily shift   substitute for your shifting
flood tide   casts a concrete floor for each day
the sound of paddling after death
this pine needle's green lifts you up and pitilessly dumps you

it's skin stripped from a zebra's face made into fields
it's a clock's flesh   seals crowd round and madly bark like shadows
eyes that see time see a window nailed shut
it's you   making the ocean old

the end   monotonous blue can't find a single word
language terminates in your language   island like a paralysed spine
October terminates in the instant that you fear the cold
nude bathing rubbing an enlarged post-mortem bruise
when the sea is endlessly crowding in on death it's more like a boundary
it's yourself revealed in your own end   it's the end
making a hundred years bright as a poisonous sparrow
because of nothing   only then engulfing you

時間海岸　（二）

我們以為早已懂得的　早已失去了
沒人能從海上回頭
目睹自己站在海岸的懸崖上
目測一滴水不可能地流入另一滴
時間在什麼時間過渡成下葬的
像影子　自陽光照射的樹身剝下
那畏懼時間的樹秘密凹陷著叢生陰毛
沒人也有影子
在死者日晷上野出的孩子
都被死者抱走

你身上流出的血才懂得拒絕你
變成別人　吸盡你

當石塊的鳥棲息在枝頭發黑
你在你四周發綠了　一根日晷上的針
靜靜籠罩古代船隊拋棄骸骨的方向
所有海　重返一個人被癌照亮的方向

我們被一切失散的繼續切割著

用制止耳鳴的瘋狂　創造這海岸
舌頭退化時　模擬一座棧橋舔食鹽類
波浪中蹬出的兔子都熟了
詩人　無力逃離一雙腳已構成罪惡

從海上回頭你看見現在是天空
肺氣腫的天空　無間隔地喘成另一片
忘卻炫耀這兒　被沒有疼痛地記著
死魚的隕石打進你的胃
狂風　給每個海岸分發足以催眠的氣候
倘若你不怕
十月就穿上觀眾醒來

The shore of time 2

what we thought we understood long ago   was long ago lost
no one can turn away from the ocean
watch yourself standing on the cliffs by the shore
visualise one drop of water flow impossibly into another
in what time is the transition between time and time's burial
like shadow   stripped from a treetrunk lit by the sunlight
the tree that dreads time secretly enfolds profuse pubic hair
no one also has a shadow
children hatched on the sundial of the dead
all carried off

the blood running from your body understands only how to refuse you
turns into someone else   sucks you dry

as birds of stone roost on the branches and blacken
you've gone green in what's all around you   a gnomon on the sundial
silently shrouding the direction of ancient armada-discarded bones
all seas   re-enter the direction of one man lit up by cancer

we're continually excised by all that's dispersed
create this shore   with a crazy gale that checks the ringing ear
when the tongue is vestigial   it's imitating a jetty licking salt
rabbits wading from the waves are done to a turn
poets powerless to escape their feet   that are crimes already

looking back from the ocean you see the now is the sky
sky of emphysema   incessantly wheezing another sky
oblivion on parade here   being painlessly remembered
meteorites of dead fish beat into your stomach
a crazy gale   hands out hypnotic weather to each shore
even if you're not afraid
October will put on an audience   and awake

POMEGRANATES DENIED

否認的石榴

紫色

時間的蛩　每年一次刺激這花朵
四肢整個是鮮豔的窗戶
讓你聽見自己在海上摔碎
樹木酷似陰影的光芒
打開陰影　佔有過去和將來的雨季
春天的鏡子從後面
看見最精緻的器官被插著
最色情的兩隻翅膀搧動一場疾病
花蕊就炫耀一剎那的死
海面上一個早晨全部被照亮的死
你身體裡的動物　比藍更紅
狂奔的牙齒　黑得像被撫摸過
越會糜爛的越在匆匆咽下性急的鮮血
殘忍　是這些花
吮吸每一滴死亡時陽光如此奪目
不得不吸　惟一可怕的
大海儲存了所有花瓣被埋葬的顏色
此刻　正順著你雙腿流下

Purple

the stalk of time   excites this flower once a year
limbs are all bright windows
letting you hear yourself shatter on the sea
trees cruelly like rays of shadow
opening shadow   owns rainy seasons past and future
from behind spring's mirror
sees the most exquisite of organs inserted
the sexiest pair of wings bringing on sickness
stamens flaunting instant death
the totally illuminated death of a morning at sea
beasts in your body   redder than blue
teeth running wild   blacken like they've been caressed
bright blood more foul the more it hurries to swallow impatience
cruelty   is these flowers
sunlight so dazzling when it sucks each drop of death
can't help sucking   the only terrible
sea stockpiles the buried colour of all petals
this moment   runs down your leg

缺席

生者身上的光已死去很久了
空白　就這樣到處被畫出
被鳥群驚恐的呼救聲圍困在中心
行走　如絕緣的天空
躍入大海的軀體　使大海變成傷口
這一筆藍就像債務的藍
這被肉體逼迫的早晨交出
一片水泥風景
暴露　你眼睛的無能

Absence

light on the bodies of the living is long dead
so blankness   is painted everywhere
pinned down in the centre by birds' startled cries
walk away   like the isolated sky
a body that leaps into the ocean   turns the ocean to a wound
this blue like the blue of debt
this flesh-compelled morning surrenders
a landscape of cement
exposes   the incompetence of your eyes

與紙垂直的方向

與紙垂直的方向上你握著
一縷早晨的煙　墓地上一顆安靜的樹
天空正在臥室中醒來
女孩們反對著　光的狂怒的莖
一枚白晝的核桃銷毀了大腦的罪證
四季　酒精持續頭疼
握緊了大海燦爛餐桌上的叉子
世界把自己的眼睛送進嘴裡

是一首從未寫完的詩
與紙垂直的　剛剛被一塊墓碑寫著
被地板上的河流流過
血液　釘成一架雙腳凍僵的梯子
被搬進搶購腐朽的擁擠隊伍
又一個早晨保持鐘錶的冷酷
垂直墜毀街頭　說
這還不是最後一次　你還沒落到紙上

Perpendicular to the paper

perpendicular to the paper you grasp
a waft of morning mist   a quiet tree in the graveyard
sky is waking in the bedroom
girls opposing   the rampant stalk of light
one little walnut of day has incinerated the brain's evidence
four seasons   alcohol sustains the headache
holds tight to the fork of the ocean's dazzling dining table
the world feeds it eyes into its mouth

it's a never-finished poem
perpendicular to the page   just being written by a headstone
floated by the floor's current
blood   hammered into a ladder of frozen feet
moved into the crowded contingent who buy up corruption
yet another morning maintains the clock's callousness
a perpendicularly crashing street   says
this isn't the last time yet   you still haven't fallen to the page

鳥之書

黑暗劇場裡　我們比那些鳥
更巨大更蒼白
把內臟翻開到外面

一本厭惡自己的書
一對翅膀發出紙聲
一隻操縱飛翔的手被光追上時是骸骨

被天空追上　被設在綠葉深處
送葬星辰的閱讀的座位觀看
死者們坐好　聆聽照耀死亡的字

狠狠釘進脊背　耳鳴一直書寫著字
墓碑的風敲打枝頭漆黑的凍梨
一本書運載著使大海陷入盲目的目的

鳥兒激怒　疲倦
使生活像一個劇本　那些活夠了的
翻開　尋找自己吞下的古老金塊

但斧頭並不選擇任何一頁
每一頁被拔光羽毛後　傷害整個天空
當我們停止鼓掌　就摔得粉身碎骨

Bird book

in the theatre of darkness   we
are bigger and paler   than these birds
our guts turned inside out

a book that detests itself
a pair of wings making paper sounds
a flight-manipulating hand is bone when caught by light

caught by sky   installed in the green leaves' depths
the reading seats of the funereal stars look on
the dead take their seats   listen with respect to words that light up death

brutally nailed to the spine   tinnitus has been writing the words all along
the headstone wind knocks the black frozen pears of the branches
a book is carrying the goal that will sink the sea in blindness

birds enraged   exhausted
make life like a script   those who have lived enough
turn inside out   seek the ancient gold they swallowed

but the axe doesn't just choose any page
after each page has had its feathers plucked away   injuring all of the sky
as we stop applauding   we fall   are dashed to pieces

鬼魂的形式

一

夏季的第一隻蟬開始哭泣
死去母親的眼睛　從未離開你
類似被稱爲夜的天空

或被稱爲白晝
或酷熱的藍是牆上純黑的大理石

一片嘴唇剛剛刻出嫩得像草
而一條舌頭脆弱得不得不呼喊
凡被喊到的　租用死者的肉體
影子再死一次　才脫落成一張人皮
小小嬰兒的白色大鳥

在樹上搧動翅膀
從光　向一片暴露你的光可怕滑行

二

末日有無數的門　讓你走向另一邊

坐在寂靜中猶如坐在雨中
被拍賣的土地　學會不呼吸地活著
把頭頂懸掛的大海注射進一千隻蘋果
死亡變甜時　天空也成熟了

假如綠色集合起所有親人的告別
四季就敞開明亮的圍牆移動一棵樹
你的恐懼把你移入課本

每天　就像死後星群不再隱去
每個人使鬼魂成爲可能的

The shape of ghosts

1

the first cicada of summer begins to weep
dead mother's eyes   have never left you
like the sky they call night

or what they call day
or sweltering blue is pure black marble on a wall

one lip has been carved tender as grass
and a tongue so vulnerable it can't help crying out
whatever was called   hired flesh from the dead
shadow dies again   is only then shed to become human skin
big white bird   tiny baby

wings of trees flapping
from light   slipping terribly towards the light that lays you bare

2

the final day has innumerable doors   makes you walk to the other side

sitting in silence is very like sitting in rain
auctioned ground   learns to live without breathing
an ocean hung by the head is injected into a thousand apples
when death turns sweet   the sky ripens too

suppose that green collected up every relatives' farewell
the seasons would open the bright wall around it to move a tree
your terror would move you into the textbook

then like the stars after death   every day would never again be hidden
and everyone would make ghosts possible

三

　　沒有。但假如鬼魂也不得不有一個人的年齡，死亡還有什麼意義？腐爛的孩子，一群群蜷縮著，組成最年幼的一個暗紅血肉。這隻落進你嘴裡的蒼蠅，是否也已上千歲？用同一個時間產卵。一枚白色顆粒埋入你肉裡照耀你。因為肉是惟一可能被照亮的。死者，喜歡一種分娩的儀式。

　　五千年的生日宴會上，你將認出，那些過去的你，和那個永遠過不去的鬼魂。互相幻想著，就像被抱著。在不可觸摸的手指溫暖觸摸中，你和你自己組成了家庭。僅僅是這具軀體，無數次被失去的地點，又都坐進忘卻那更黑的石頭小廣場，被留下。沒有。疼痛。一千年長達一次抽搐。

四

　　　　是　死亡那類似母親的眼睛
　　　　薰香了樹木
　　　　是母親眼中的死亡誕生一首夏天的詩
　　　　這紫色花朵一直盛開到你的終點
　　　　純黑大理石的反光　讓你死在起點
　　　　是你自己在天空深處集體性交
　　　　是瘋子　被瘋狂無盡地挖掘成倒影

　　　　當一剎那你看見石頭那邊的你

　　　　海洋嗅出了最乏味的瞎子
　　　　光有受傷的腳趾時　藍必然不是一滴水
　　　　兩面相對流走的鏡子間沒有出路

　　　　永遠不會有
　　　　當人是鬼魂最簡單的形式　夏天
　　　　就保持燦爛　以一場吞吃母親的疾病
　　　　當鬼魂比一切花朵更是孤兒
　　　　你無望地被自己眼中的死亡誕生了

　　　　蟬　在體內叫個不停

no. but supposing ghosts can't help having the age that people have either, would death still have any meaning? rotted children, huddled together in flocks, would make up the dull red flesh of the youngest. is the fly that falls into your mouth thousands of years old too? it laid its eggs in identical time. a tiny white grain buried in your flesh illuminates you. because flesh is the only thing that can be lit up. the dead, they like a ceremony for childbirth.

at a five-thousandth birthday party, you will recognise all those yous of the past, and the ghost that can never pass away. dreaming each other, like an embrace. under the warm touch of a finger that cannot touch, you and your self have formed a family. it can only be this body, a place lost innumerable times, and they're both sitting in the little stone plaza that has forgotten that deeper black, left behind. no. pain. a thousand years lengthen into one convulsion.

4

yes   death the mother-like eye
has perfumed the tree
it's death in a mother's eye that gives birth to a poem of summer
this purple flower has bloomed all the way to your end
reflection of pure black marble   makes you die at your start
it's yourself having an orgy in the depths of the sky
it's a madman   endlessly dug into a reflection by madness

in the instant you see the you in the other side of that stone

the ocean has smelt out the dullest of blind men
when light's toes are wounded   blue cannot be a drop of water
between two mirrors that flow in opposing directions there's no escape

there never can be
when we are the simplest of a soul's shapes   summer
sustains splendour   with a sickness that eats mothers
when souls are lonelier than every flower
you are hopelessly born from the death in your own eyes

cicadas   in the body   endlessly cry

蛇樹

1

致命的想像移植到窗外
此刻　花園是劇毒天空的一部分
綠色完成於一場洪水
泡漲的馬　或啄食腐爛腸子的烏鴉
孩子盯著樹說　蛇
陽光遲鈍的聽覺裡響起嘶嘶聲

2

風暴使你活著
風暴　抽打蛇身的藝人
雙重虛構的樹枝
尾巴在一根刺耳的笛子上打成死結
如一群抓住子宮不放的辛辣胎兒

3

掰開春天長鱗的　渾身唾液的
用腹部滑行的手指

4

從哪兒開始　這是樹　而那是蛇
從一個死者到另一個死者
肉體內部的大雪怎樣忍受脫皮的疼痛
落到外面

Snake tree

1

fatal fancy grafted beyond the window
this instant   the garden is part of a toxic sky
green perfected in a flood
swollen horse   or crow pecking at rotting guts
a child stares at a tree and says   snakes
a fizzing in sunlight's torpid ears

2

storm brings you alive
storm   artist lashing the snakes
twice-fictional branches
tails sealed knots on shrill flutes
like acrid embryos imprisoned in the womb

3

finger
that prises spring's scales open   that's covered in spittle
that slides on its belly

4

where to begin   these are trees   and those are snakes
from one dead person to another
how does the snow of the body's insides bear the pain of sloughing skin
falling outside

5

花園　是一首劇毒的詩的一部分
所有天氣都剛剛被折疊過
所有樹　跟隨一棵正被孵化成蛇類的
一個孩子眼睛裡恐怖的就是好玩的
你含在咽喉深處的牙
杜撰那鳥鳴　被按進墨綠沼澤的
夜空　與一片藍相反爬動
自願飢餓的辭結滿瘋狂的果實

6

每分鐘裡多少次呼吸
每次呼吸中多少棵蛇樹
每顆蛇樹上多少酷愛幻想死亡的器官

7

惡高懸於內心的形式　聚集著土地
樹枝在你的堅持下繼續長出
向下彎曲　切除包皮的純肉棍子
抽著不怕毒死的芽
四季　闡釋一種多天陰冷的美學
冷血滲入任何一個脆弱骨節
風中退化的腳　糾纏如舌頭
詩人就還在捋光葉子
裸露的蛇更殘忍時只是一株植物
用關於孩子的聯想
把孩子扎穿
像一棵蛇樹閒暇中偶然完成的

5

the garden   is part of a toxic poem
all the weather has just been folded up
all the trees   follow
what hatched into a snake
what was fear in a child's eyes   was fun
teeth held deep in your throat
inventing that birdsong   night sky
pressed down into a green-black swamp
crawling in opposition to a piece of blue
freely famished words
tied up in fruits of madness

6

in every minute how many breaths
in every breath how many snake trees
in every snake tree how many organs that yearn for death

7

shape that sin hangs in the innermost heart   gathering ground
a tree continually growing from under your persistence
curling down   a circumcising rod of pure flesh
putting out a bud that fears no poison
four seasons   expound a sombre aesthetic of winter
cold blood seeps into any fragile joint
feet regressing in the wind   tangled as tongues
and the poet still stripping the leaves
when the stripped snake is more cruel it's just a plant
using associations of childhood
to run the child through
like a snake tree accidentally achieved in leisure

收割

這些經過脫粒的　燙手的屋頂
在夏季的場院上發亮
這些被自己曝曬的天空突然變黑

海縮小　銀白刺眼的瓦
兩棵樹相對奔跑
兩次飢饉　用一個人的麥子播種

明年的死亡也已過時
陽光撞斷了脖子
你的眼睛　碾平暴露狂的城市

Harvest

these husked   scalding rooftops
shine on the threshing floor of summer
these self-sunblasted skies suddenly blacken

the sea shrinks   glaringly bright silver tiles
two trees rush off in opposite directions
two famines   sown in one man's corn

next year's death already past
sunlight has broken its neck
your eyes   flatten the city of flashers

最簡單的

食肉的魚呲出一口牙微笑
月亮　卻像個被射中的越獄者
臉朝下死去

從影子上撕下光
從光　撕下這隻被光誘騙的豚鼠

河水一直沸騰
四條小腿　拼命划動中只剩下白骨
鮮血的最後一身皮毛緊緊懷抱
眼睛還瞪著天空　不知誰活活被吃掉

The simplest thing

a piranha bares a mouthful of smiling teeth
but the moon   like a shot jailbreaker
dies face down

tear off light from shade
from light   tear off this guinea-pig inveigled by the light

the river has been raging
four little legs   white bones all that's left of the desperate paddling
the last skin of blood tightly clasps its body
eyes still stare at the sky   not knowing who's eating it alive

節日

陽光驅逐你　而黑暗打開它的灌木
詩人死於車禍
詩　殘廢於彩色膠印的天空

一直敲響的鐘聲像件瘋狂的禮物
孩子夢見手心的小小地洞裡
有條多眠的蛇
慘白的霧試探著入口

與天堂相反的方向　卻不配
稱為地獄

Fiesta

sunlight chases you away   and darkness opens its bushes
the poet dies in a car crash
poetry   maimed in a colour-printed sky

the continual knocking of bells is like an insane gift
children dream of hibernating snakes
in the tiny hole of the palm
pallid mist probing the entrance

the opposite direction from heaven
doesn't deserve   to be called hell

公園

春天的權力　是再次
遠遠扔出一根黑色樹枝

風暴中的海象
癱瘓在長椅上呲著牙齒

北極總會用想像的綠
建造停放屍首的房子

說　看看這歡樂
一條上了當狂奔而去的狗

Park

the powers of spring   once again
fling out a black branch

a walrus in the storm
paralysed on a bench   is baring its teeth

the north pole can always use the green of imagination
to build a house to keep corpses in

speak   see this joy
a dog tricked into running madly away

大學

我們在麵包上均勻塗抹一代人的果醬
風　和女孩淡紅的小腿
被夾進餓狼縮不回爪子的目光

嚼

假牙耀眼的白擴散到血液裡
陽光繼續磨損站滿天空的古老雕像
打樁機的頭一下一下點著

吞咽

翅膀上修剪整齊的肉
講課聲的毛巾被喉嚨擰乾
草地　就為午餐

擦嘴

擦拭準時的知識
互相校正一條勒在手腕上的蛇
當畢業典禮的人造大理石

排泄

出賣手淫的年齡
濺滿鮮桔汁的黑色袍袖比噩夢更臃腫
毀滅　在一隻被毀滅的胃裡成熟

University

we are spreading the jam of a generation onto bread
wind   and girls' pink calves
are squeezed into a hungry wolf's unflinching gaze

chewing

the bright white of false teeth is diffused into the blood
sunlight goes on grinding the ancient statues that stand all around the sky
pile-driver head nodding with each blow

swallowing

neatly clipped flesh of wings
the sound of teaching is a towel wrung dry by the throat
for lunch   the lawn

wiping its mouth

wiping punctual knowledge clean
adjusts the snake tied round the wrist
as people made marble at graduation

excreting

sells up the age of masturbation
sleeves of black gowns splattered with fresh orange juice
more bloated than nightmares
ruin   ripening in a ruined stomach

水泥人

1

非人的月光　再萎縮就成了人造的
四季天藍色的肉　失血
成爲終年的灰
孩子奔跑是必死的象徵

2

死者被四肢裡的積雪磨著
一口水泥棺材
把活的鳥兒變成釘子
野貓盤旋在高處草叢中
勤奮發情的骯髒天鵝
掀開每天的水泥被子

3

跑到哪兒　不跑到哪兒　跑不到哪兒

不得不跑

渾身關緊夜的窗戶
壁虎畢生爬一堵骸骨的牆
大海更深地漏出沙子
石頭的恥辱　是忍受微弱的心跳聲

4

天空的手就要狠狠拍下
呼救總晚一點　比死亡只晚一點

你還在玩木頭人遊戲
你住進地下室才追上你自己

Cement man

1

the inhuman moonlight   withers again to become the man-made
meat of four sky-blue seasons   blood loss
becomes year-round grey
the running of children an emblem of certain death

2

the dead are ground down by mantling snow in the limbs
a cement coffin
turns living birds to nails
wild cats circle in high thickets
dirty swans in diligent heat
tear open the cement coverlet of each day

3

where to run   where not to run   where can't you run

can't not run

whole body shut tight in the window of night
lifelong the lizard climbs a wall of bones
the ocean leaks more deeply from the sand
a stone's shame   is to endure the sound of feeble heartbeats

4

the sky's hand will mercilessly slap down
cries for help always a little late   later only than death

you're still playing at statues
you can only catch up with yourself
when you live in the cellar

中世紀聖像畫

平靜地接受死亡已是很久以前的事
當一個名字抵消一種智慧
肉體　最後忍受著受難的金色

每個嬰兒學會用哭聲爭論
關於黑夜的哲學
是否總多於所有黑夜

安魂曲唱不出傷口之外的
筆觸也畫不出
任何一雙眼睛的暴露狂

深邃的天空拒絕一個人墜入
從那時到現在　我們
發明的　只有嘴和耳膜間冗長的距離

Portrait of a medieval saint

calm acceptance of death happened long ago
when a name cancels out a kind of wisdom
flesh   accepts at last the gold of suffering

every infant learns how to use weeping
to dispute whether the philosophies of night
are always more than nights themselves

a requiem can't sing what is beyond wounds
nor brushstrokes paint
the indecent exposure of the eyes

the profound sky permits no falling into it
since then   what we have invented
is only the redundant distance between ear and eye

歌劇

歌聲緩緩退回下午的最後一排座位
我們在赤裸的天空赤裸著
再坦白一點就是鳥　渾身金黃地飛過
衰老的耳朵裡沒有年輕的音色
這是春天　春天最適於去死
去閱讀任何一本書的悲劇

也許沉默能把故事再講一次
天堂的火焰　雖然可怕也是擁抱
給這窗口一大把肉色花朵
給眺望的下午一片不停墜落的海
金屬的風暴　把疼痛鑄造在聽覺裡
讓我們冷卻得像孩子
用來不及訣別的暮色與天空訣別
但天空　說出過什麼

黑夜轉過身子
黑暗是荒涼的後台

Opera

the sound of singing unhurriedly returns to the afternoon's last seat
we are naked beneath the naked sky
most candid again are the birds   flying by all golden yellow
no youthful timbres in decrepit ears
this is spring   spring is the perfect time to die
to read any book's tragedy

if silence can tell a story over again
the flame of heaven   embracing though terrifying
gives this window a bunch of flesh-coloured flowers
gives the onlooking afternoon an endlessly falling sea
the golden storm   forges pain in the hearing
let us chill like children
use a twilight too late for goodbyes to say goodbye to the sky
but the sky   what did it say

night has turned its back
darkness is a bleak backstage

博物館

孤獨並非最後的據點　它什麼也不是
純粹的死亡猶如擺在大廳裡的花朵
鮮豔　脖子被剪斷
一個三月淡淡散發出甜味兒
血應當被忽略　因而更像傑作

並非燈光代替了陽光照耀
這根黃金的枝條才乾枯

黑夜與黑夜的大理石牆壁　被磨亮
鳥叫聲的青銅斧頭劈下時
從未降落的雨　佈置天空僅有的內容
和我們　一個順從移動的話題
更悠閒地坐在畫外
看著自己被大師刮掉

Museum

loneliness isn't the final stronghold   it is nothing
pure death is like the flowers arranged in the hall
blazing with colour   throats cut
the subtle sweetness emitted by March
blood should be ignored   so it's more like a masterpiece

if lamplight hadn't replaced the sun
this branch of gold would have withered

the marble wall of night and night   is polished and shining
when the bronze axe of birdsong strikes
never-fallen rain   spreads out the only content of the sky
and we   a topic amenable to motion
sit more idly outside the painting
watching ourselves scraped away by a master's hand

隱喻

然後　天空的罪惡依舊繁衍到你身上
一根綠色樹枝捕食鳥類
一個黃昏決心蓋緊音箱
爲什麼不彈奏
任何一片黑暗從來不是殘缺的
有歌劇　角色就不開口
河　把岸上的行人變成溺水者
橋架在你體內
你得走向一直迴避的那個終點
被不屑於忘記你的日子再忘一次
月光　過去了的才是透明的
讓你愛這不得不恨的風景
休止
靜得聽見了全部音樂

Metaphor

afterwards   as always the sky's crimes breed on your body
a green branch preying on birds
a twilight deciding to switch off the speakers
why don't they play?
no darkness has ever been a fragment
there is opera   a role doesn't open its mouth
a river   turns passers-by on its banks into drowning men
the bridge's span inside your body
you must head for that endpoint you've always avoided
forgotten again by days that disdain to forget you
moonlight   only transparent once it's gone
makes you love a landscape you have to hate
pause
so silent you have heard all music

史前

日子摘下日子的面具　還剩什麼
拍打你後背的保姆
仍是充滿謀殺慾的天空

窗戶　比鯊魚的牙更古老
失傳時看到海
一條狠狠舔入旅遊指南的藍色舌頭
刺激得沙灘上的肉一絲不掛
炎熱中　死亡在加速

一絲風就能搖晃這個世界
末日的風　誰是最後剩下的孩子
任何一張臉遮住臉後的岩石
就在史前　重演一雙手餵養的饑餓
海塵土飛揚
站在蜘蛛的腿上
一棵明亮的樹掛滿鮮花的魚餌
誘騙　早被誘騙過千年的
你

Prehistory

the day takes off the mask of the day   what's left there
a nanny who slaps your back
a sky still full of murderous intent

a window   more ancient than shark's teeth
when it's lost to history   it looks at the sea
a blue tongue that mercilessly licks into the guidebook
so turned on that the flesh on the beach is utterly naked
in the blazing heat   death is speeding up

a breath of wind can rock this world
the wind of the last days   who will be the last child left?
any face hides the stone behind a face
so recurs in prehistory   a famine fed by one pair of hands
the dust of the sea flying
standing on spider's legs
a bright tree all hung with bait of flowers
to deceive   the thousands of years ago-deceived
you

空間

鳥狂熱地排擠空氣
吱吱響的海面　透明彎曲的玻璃

被蘋果樹看護著
朗誦的蘋果　一個綠色的鴇母

支持花朵冒煙
形成一匹馬雪白的斑點

整座城市急速向後崩潰
夏季的鮮艷花園　一隻死蝴蝶

埋進汗水和陰毛裡的嘴
如此精緻地向手錶報仇

兩列火車開出肉體
準時在一個字中迎面相撞

正午　被記憶放棄的藍色田野
停在男人禿頂上持續轟炸

當死亡的毛衣突然縮水
地獄　小得躺不下兩個人

Space

birds feverishly push the air aside
the sea's sighing surface   clear sinuous glass

protected by the apple tree
a much-praised apple   a green bawd

supporting the smoking flowers
taking the shape of a horse's snow-white dappling

suddenly the whole city collapses backwards
summer's brilliant garden   a dead butterfly

so mouths buried in sweat and pubic hair
take exquisite revenge on the clock

two trains drive the bodies out
punctually collide head-on in a word

noon   a blue field abandoned by memory
stops its continuous bombardment of a bald head

as death's sweater shrinks
hell   is so tiny we can't both lie down

被終止的

這首驚動老虎的詩　不得不終止在
一張自肘部逃離的桌子上
辭與辭的風暴從來是告別的

土地　在移動的紅色條紋下移動
每天的白色樹幹脫光肉質的葉子
你用膝蓋感到那老虎
穿過你　把星星吞入黑暗的腹中

不會飛翔的頭顱　反襯著鳥
淹死在湖底的孩子　充實月光的背景
被更換的僅僅是睡眠
道路上的睡眠　紫色的小小內臟夢見松鼠
軀體外的睡眠　再次把軀體留在原地
學習更惡毒的神
不死　游行　沒有終止才最後終止

收藏老虎的石頭
你以為你真的在移動
而不是瞎了癱瘓在
每一個被迫杜撰的腳步上嗎

What ended

this poem that disturbs the tiger   has to end on
a table that flees from the elbows
the storm of word and word always told goodbye

earth   always moving under a moving red stripe
each day's white tree trunks stripped of fleshy leaves
with your knees you feel the tiger
pass through you   swallow the stars into the belly of darkness

a skull that cannot soar   sets off the birds
a child drowned on a lake bed   enriches the moonlit background
what's renewed is simply sleep
sleep on the road   tiny purple organs dream of squirrels
sleep outside the body   leave the body in its place again and again
learn to be a more vicious god
continue parading without death   no end is the final end

stone that collects the tigers
you think you really are moving
but isn't it blinded paralysis at
every step you're forced to fabricate

北方

田野乘著雪橇　無聲地滑入過去
道路　僅僅證實天空在崩潰
像每個字背後用盡的白

時間　裸露
零度時淡紅色灌木抽打春天的激情

一扇窗戶比一隻野兔奔跑更急速
你被移開　塞進一具兔毛脫落的軀體
兩耳被白色足跡拎著
光　死死釘在寒冷的方向
一種精緻得人類不認識的病
你不看　野兔的內臟也遮住地平線
發炎　大笑
徹底消失於一場不變的雪

如果記憶存在　你被切下時更完美

The North

fields are sledging   silently slipping into the past
the road   simply confirms that the sky is crumbling
like the used white behind every letter

time   laid bare
down to zero   pale red brushwood's zeal for drubbing spring

a window runs faster than a rabbit
you are diverted   stuffed into a body shorn of rabbit fur
ears lifted by white footprints
light   nailed firmly in the direction of cold
a sickness so exquisite it's unknown to humans
you don't see   the rabbit's organs hide the horizon too
inflammation   laughter
utterly vanish in unchanging snow

if memory exists   you are more perfect when you are cut down

南方

大海用子宮中每一塊肌肉收縮的力量
否認著大海　活魚被油煎的刺痛
否認死亡僅僅是空虛的
頭上的藍色書籍　被盲人否認了
陽光炫耀一個騎馬女孩的性
而海灘上暗綠的下肢傳播謠言

當十二個月的夏季不否認對你的憎恨
你的一生　是否足夠否認這一天

一張放在履歷中的桌子
使你走不出這酷熱
一具屍體被蒸熟　繼續碰撞你的夜
大汗淋漓的雲弄濕一部字典
空中解體的臃腫魚類　被沒寫的
寫進你從未到達的腳下這一頁
被飛翔再否認一次

繁殖更差的　更明亮　更易於毀滅

The South

the ocean uses the strength of every contraction in the womb
to deny the ocean   the stabbing pain of live fish frying
denying death is simply inane
the blue books on the head   denied by blind men
sunlight illuminates the young horsewoman's sex
but dark green legs on the beach spread rumours

if the twelve-month summer doesn't deny it hates you
is your whole life   enough to deny this one day?

a desk put into your cv
leaves you unable to escape this cruel heat
a corpse steamed tender   keeps colliding with your night
sweat-soaked clouds drench the dictionary
bloated fish dismembered in air   are written by what's unwritten
into the page beneath your foot which you never reach
denied yet again by soaring

more defectively breeding   brighter   more easily destroyed

其他沒有的

語言　死在陳述裡
紫色結晶的大海死在一個別處的湖裡
儲存於孕婦嘔吐聲中的世界
讓胎兒記起了　天空藍得像牙疼

呼吸　精密得像一枚炸彈的定時裝置

一下午的黃金在熔化博物館的窗子
死亡的中心廣場　死在你眼裡
看著不可觸及的雪落下
多天落下　沒有的已成為每天的
被肉體無知的溫度兇狠報復

大海　每天重返懷裡一根白骨
你每天瘋狂回憶一個現實

擦掉一個辭　樹死在風的地址上
胎兒的頭死了才綠了
只剩笑聲　才照亮腐爛清晰的刻度
你逼近你中心那沒有的方向
海也不可觸及了　覆蓋別處的雪
突然覆蓋到處

沒有一隻鳥沒有俯衝進如此舊的血跡

Others that are not

language   dies in statements
the purple crystal ocean dies in a lake elsewhere
a world stored up in the sound of morning sickness
makes an embryo recall   a sky blue as toothache

breathing   accurate as a bomb's timing device

the gold of an afternoon is dissolving in the window of a museum
death's central square   dies in your eye
watching the untouchable snow fall
winter falls   what is not has become what's everyday
a savage reprisal by the body's ignorant temperature

the ocean   re-enters every day a white bone in the breast
every day you insanely remember a reality

erase a word   a tree dies at the wind's address
the embryo's head only green after death
only laughter left   to light up clear gradations of corruption
you draw near your centre   that direction which is not
the sea too is untouchable   snow that covers elsewhere
suddenly covers everywhere

no bird that hasn't dived into bloodstains this old

追憶

鳥類的白色狼群狂奔在雪地上
月光　低聲咆哮中
天空摘下天空的面具

星群　炸裂於樹梢的高度
液體悲慘地滲出
一口隱匿生命的井

一根刺比秋天疼得更長久
盯著黑暗的銀幕
記住　垂直陷落的墓穴如今夜

Looking back

a white wolfpack of birds runs madly over the snow
moonlight   in a quiet roar
the sky takes off the mask of the sky

constellations   explode at treetop height
liquids tragically leak out
a well that hides lives

a thorn whose pain lasts longer than autumn
staring at the dark screen
remember   the grave is vertically sunk   so is tonight

玻璃藝人

被時間切割是唯一的快感
你一生等待　玻璃指甲慢慢長出
玻璃的根扎進一個大海

黑暗　就像老化的藍
孩子　在自己臉上摸到死亡
一件傑作中摸不到的光
使一隻鳥的小小瓶子盛滿四季的水

如此易碎
誰在過去成形就躍入冷卻的　肯定的

玻璃的愛情　使大海無力翻動
鈴聲搭成這個鳥巢
你全部的虛耗　僅僅是一天
今天　被不變的風暴確認爲死過的
不怕腐爛的　在陽光中閉緊眼睛

Glassblower

being sliced by time is the only delight
you wait all your life   for the slow growth of glass nails
glass roots stuck in an ocean

the darkness   like ageing blue
a child   touches death in his own face
the untouchable light in a masterpiece
fills the little bottle of a bird with the water of four seasons

so fragile
who was formed by the past leaps into what's frozen   what's affirmed

love of glass   makes the ocean weakly ripple
tinkling bells built into this bird's nest
all of your worst   is only one day
today   is what's confirmed by the unchanging storm to have died
is what fears no corruption   has its eyes tightly shut in the sunlight

復仇的蝴蝶

一隻被你毒死的蝴蝶有一張人臉
烏黑陰郁的翅膀　必定有記憶
記得　最後一次俯衝時女性的瘋狂

仇恨　認出自己是花朵
早晨明亮的錯覺中
一隻黑色粉撲　撲滿噩夢的鮮艷房間
蝴蝶又等在你怕看的牆上

被你親手撕毀後　找到你
被變成陰影　用風聲觸目地包圍
一張細細咬你的嘴　在死後

必定是人的　反向佔領綠色的天空
你越想忘記越明白蝴蝶在復仇

Butterfly of revenge

the butterfly you poisoned had a human face
gloomy jet-black wings   are bound to have memory
remember   the feminine madness of its last dive toward you

hatred   thinks itself a flower
in the misconceptions of bright morning
a black powder-puff   puffs the gaudy room full of nightmare
again the butterfly waits on the wall you fear to see

shredded by your hand   it finds you
turned to shadow   shockingly surrounded by the wind's voice
a tiny mouth that bites you   after death

it's bound to belong to someone   invading the green sky backwards
the more you want to forget
the more you see the butterfly is taking its revenge

布萊希特的最後提問

冬天意味著發黑的松樹
雪　意味著沒有人的房間裡
從早到晚的燈光

照耀　有人的墓地
卸了妝的骷髏使你更像詩人
把上一個群眾角色的一生脫在窗外

意味著參觀自己冰冷的笑
玻璃的封面　內容是一場暴風雪
死亡的劇目　一座城市的菜譜

讓鐘聲在兩個終點間像掌聲
兩個你　互相被想像
手的醜陋鳥兒書寫灰暗天空的贗品

意味著死者早已看到了
這墓碑站在書房窗外　像個弔唁的字
每一根松針的綠最後被租用

讓敵對的　現存的
整個完美無缺的黃昏虛擬你的瘋狂
問　夜有什麼　夜死過兩次還奢望什麼

Brecht's last question

winter signifying blackening pine trees
snow   signifying in an unoccupied room
lamplight from morning to night

lighting up   an occupied graveyard
a disrobed skull makes you more like a poet
taking off outside the window the public role of your last life

signifying a visit to your own frozen smile
the binding of glass   the contents a snowstorm
death's repertoire   a menu of the city

let the bell's song between both your endpoints be handclaps
two of you   imagining each other
ugly birds of hands writing the phoney grey sky

it signifies the dead have long ago seen
this headstone outside the study window   like a letter of condolence
the green of every pine needle finally rented out

let the antagonistic   the extant
the whole flawless twilight invent your madness
ask   what has night got
night has died twice   what can it still hope for

WHERE THE SEA
STANDS STILL

大海停止之處

大海停止之處

1

藍總是更高的　當你的厭倦選中了
海　當一個人以眺望迫使海
倍加荒涼

依舊在返回
這石刻的耳朵裡鼓聲毀滅之處
珊瑚的小小屍體　落下一場大雪之處

死魚身上鮮艷的斑點
像保存你全部性欲的天空

返回一個界限　像無限
返回一座懸崖　四周風暴的頭顱
你的管風琴注定在你死後
繼續演奏　肉裡深藏的腐爛的音樂

當藍色終於被認出　被傷害
大海　用一萬枝蠟燭奪目地停止

Where the sea stands still

1

blue is always higher   just as your weariness has chosen
the sea   just as a man's gaze compels the sea
to be twice as desolate

going back as ever
to that carved stone ear where drumbeats are destroyed
where tiny coral corpses   fall in a snowstorm

gaudy speckles on dead fish
like the sky that holds all your lust

go back to the limit   like limitlessness
going back to the cliffs   stormheads all around
your pipes doomed to go on playing
after your death   tunes of corruption deep in the flesh

as blue is recognised at last   the wounded
sea   a million candles   stands dazzlingly still

現實　再次貶低詩人的瘋狂
一個孩子有權展示一種簡短的死
火焰使眾多軀體下降到零度
恨　團結了初春的灰燼
花蕊噴出的濃煙　越是寧靜越是傲慢

一廂情願的純潔的恐怖
這一天　已用盡了每天的慘痛
火　嗆進肺葉時
海水　看到母親從四肢上紛紛蒸發
去年的花園在海上擰乾自己

在海鷗茫然的叫聲中上升到極點
孩子們犯規的死亡
使死亡　代表一個春天扮演了
偶然的仇敵　黑暗中所有來世的仇敵
僅僅因為拒絕在此刻活著

2

reality   belittles the madness of poets again
a child has the right to reveal a brief death
flame brings crowds of bodies back down to zero
hate   has united the ashes of early spring
thick smoke spat from stamens   grows prouder still in tranquillity

the pure terror of your wish
this one day   has used up each day's bitter grief
when fire   chokes the lung's lobes
seawater   watches mother's limbs swirl and evaporate
last year's garden is squeezed out on the sea

rising to the zenith through the blank cries of seagulls
the non-licit deaths of young children
make death   understudy for spring
a chance enmity   the enmity of all your future in the darkness
because of a refusal to live in this moment

單調的與被單調重複的　是罪行
一個獨處懸崖的人比懸崖更像盡頭
你　被上千噸藍色石塊砸著
眼睛　躲不開砸來的大海
那看見白晝的與被白晝剝光的
時間　死者放肆的色情

一根魚骨被打磨得更尖不可能是錯誤

一滴血　稀釋了懷抱沉船的水
象牙過時而殘忍像一座陽台
樹木　又網住自己枝頭綠色的魚群

這間雪白病房裡　雪白的是繁殖
乳房袒露在屋頂上　狂風
改變每隻不夠粗暴的手
天空的兩腿被床欄固定

給了海　大海在睡夢中更無知地滑動
一隻蟑螂抽搐得酷似人類

過去的與被過去吐出的　只是肉
這現實　被你記起　只有遠去的肉
否定一座藍色懸崖
否定了翅膀的大海早已被摔碎
你臉上　每個波浪寫下光的謊言的傳記
而盯著盡頭的眼睛是一隻鮮牡蠣
正無盡地返回隔夜壞死之處

3

what's drab and what's drably copied   is criminal
someone living alone on a cliff is closer to the edge than the cliffs are
you   are battered by a thousand tons of blue rock
eyes   can't dodge the ocean's battering
what watches the day and what's stripped bare by the day
time   the hardcore pornography of the dead

a fishbone polished still sharper can never be wrong

a drop of blood   has diluted waters that embrace sunken ships
ivory archaic and ruthless as a balcony
trees   net green shoals in their branches again

in this snow-white sickroom   that white is breeding
breasts bared on rooftops   gales
change each hand too gentle
the sky's legs pinned down by the bedrail

for the sea   the ocean slides more dumbly in dreams
a cockroach twitches terribly like a human

what's past and what's spat out by the past   is only flesh
in this reality   you called to memory   there's only faraway flesh
rejecting blue cliffs
the sea that rejected wings is smashed to pieces
on your face   the lying biography each wave writes with light
and an eye staring at the edge is a fresh oyster
where the necrosis of last night goes endlessly back

大海停止之處

1

鋪柏油的海面上一隻飛鳥白得像幽靈

嗅到岸了　那燈塔就停在
左邊　我們遇難之處

鋪柏油的海面上一隻錨是崩斷的犁

一百年　以墓碑陡峭的程度
刷新我們的名字
在紅色岩石的桌子旁被看著就餐
海水　碧綠松針的籌火讓骸骨取暖
呲出滿口鏽蝕發黑的牙　跳舞

小教堂的尖頂被夾進每個八月的這一夜
死亡課上必讀的暴風雨

那光就停在　更多死者聚集之處
錨鏈斷了　錨墜入嬰兒的號哭深處
情人們緊緊摟抱在柏油下

一百年才讀懂一隻表漆黑的內容

Where the sea stands still

1

on the tarmac sea a ghost-white bird

smells its way to the shore   the lighthouse sticks
at the left   the place where we met our untimely end

on the tarmac sea an anchor is a broken plough

with the leaning of tombstones   a century
rewrites our names
seen beside the table of red rock as we dine
on seawater   the green bonfire of pine needles warming the skeleton
baring a rust-blackened mouthful of teeth   dancing

the little church steeple squeezes into this night each August
a storm   required reading in death's lesson

light stops   where more dead congregate
the anchor chain has snapped   the anchor sunk deep where infants wail
lovers clasped tight beneath the tar

after a century we grasped the blackness of the clock

2

花朵的工事瞄準了大海
一隻等待落日的啤酒杯　塗滿金黃色
像嘴唇上逐漸加重的病情
那說話的　在玻璃中繼續說話

那歌唱的　都被一把電吉他唱出
用十倍的音量封鎖一個聾子
微笑　就是被錄製的
食物　掰開手指

水手溺死的側影　就逼近
在椅子和椅子之間變成複數
風和風是呼吸之間一灘鹹腥的血跡
那被稱為人的　使辭語遍布裂縫

石頭雪白的腳踝原地踏步
使心跳的樓梯癱瘓
日子　既不上升也不下降就抵達了
最後的　醉鬼的　被反芻的　海

the flower's defences have the ocean in their sights
a beerglass waits for sunset   to paint gold and yellow
like a steadily sinking disease on the lips
that talker   still talking through the glass

that singer   electrocuted into song
at ten-fold volume to seal up the deaf
smile   is recorded
food   breaks fingers off

drowned silhouette of a sailor   presses in
multiplies between chair and chair
between in-breath and out wind on wind is a rank salt beach of bloodstains
that one called a man   makes words split and crack

stone's snow-white heels stamp on the primal earth
paralyse the stairway of heartbeats
the days   since they neither ascend nor descend   have reached
the final   drunken   cud-chewed   sea

麻痺的與被麻痺裹脅的年齡
沉船裡的年齡
這忘記如何去疼痛的肉體敞開皮膚
終於被大海摸到了內部

被洗淨的肝臟一隻白色水母
被醃熟的臉　牽制著上千顆星星
被海龜佔領的床　仍演奏發亮的樂器

當月光無疑是我們的磷光
潮汐　不停地刮過更年幼的子宮
呼救停進　所有不存在的聽覺

在　鯊魚被血激怒前靜靜懸掛的一剎那

我們不動　天空就堆滿鐵銹
我們被移動　大海的紫色陰影緊握著
一百年　一雙噴吐墨汁的手
摸　無力的與被無力實現的睡眠
恥辱　騎在燈塔上
摸　死者爲沙灘遺留的自瀆的肉體
飛鳥小小的弓把飛翔射入那五指
我們的靈柩不得不追隨今夜

挖掘　被害那無底的海底
停止在一場暴風雨不可能停止之處

3

paralysed years and years forced in by paralysis
years in sunken ships
this flesh which has forgotten how to banish pain opens wide its skin
insides finally touched by the ocean

liver washed clean, a single white jellyfish
face pickled   pinning down a thousand stars
bed captured by a turtle   still playing a shining instrument

as moonlight is clearly our phosphorescence
tides   endlessly scrape younger wombs clean
cries for help cease in   all the ears not there

in   a quietly suspended moment before the shark's feeding frenzy

we don't shift   rust piles up over the sky
we're shifted   the ocean's purple shadow tightly clasps
a century   a pair of hands spit ink
touch   powerless and powerlessly attained sleep
shame   riding on a lighthouse
touches   the masturbating flesh that the dead bequeath the beach
wheeling birds are tiny bows that shoot into five fingers
our coffins compelled to pursue this night

dig it out   that bottomless wounded seabed   stands still
where a storm can never stand

大海停止之處

1

誰和你在各自的死亡中互相瀕臨
誰說　惟一被豐收的石頭
使海沉入你的水下
當你看時　只能聽到鳥聲就是葬禮
你聽　卻夢見海的暗紅封面
攤在窗台上
噩夢把你更挑剔地讀完
屍首們被再次回憶起來的白堊填滿了
誰和你分享這痛哭的距離

現在是最遙遠的

你的停止有大海瘋狂的容量
孤獨的容量　讓一隻耳朵冥想
每個乾枯貝殼裡猛獸的鮮血在流盡
雪白劇毒的奶　一滴就足夠
給你的陽光哺乳

睜開眼睛就淪為現實
閉緊　就是黑暗的同類

Where the sea stands still

1

who comes with you close to each of your deaths
who says   the one harvested stone
makes the sea sink to the level of your water
as you look   you can only hear birdsong as funeral music
you listen   but dream of the ocean's carmine dustjacket
placed on the windowsill
picky nightmares read you more closely still
corpses stuffed with recalled-again chalk
who shares this doleful distance with you

now is furthest away

your standstill is as full as the ocean's madness
the fullness of solitude   makes an ear think long
in every dry shell predators have been drained of fresh blood
snow-white poison milk   one drop enough
to suckle your sunlight

eyes open and fall into reality
shut tight   is kin to the dark

2

這類似死亡的一剎那　激情的一剎那
黑色床單上的空白同時在海上
中斷的一剎那　肉體
用肉體的鏡子逃出了自己
焚燒的器官是一條走廊
而癱瘓　是使大海耀眼的湛藍目的
女孩們歡呼放棄　停止存在時
最鮮嫩的窗戶都濕漉漉被海推開

投入一個方向　沒有的方向
遠離彈奏的手指　琴本身就是音樂
遠離風　鹽住進全部過去的傷
類似被遺忘的僅僅是現在
正午的黑色床單上一片空白性慾的水
血緣越遠越燦爛　照亮了墮落的一剎那
現在裡沒有時間　沒人慢慢醒來
說　除了幻象沒有海能活著

2

this death-like instant   this instant of passion
this instant simultaneously blank on the black bedsheet
and suspended on the sea   flesh
escapes itself through the mirror of flesh
the blazing organ is a corridor
paralysis   the bright blue goal that makes the ocean dazzle
girls urgently cry for rest   when being stands still
the tenderest windows are damp, pushed open by the sea

fling yourself in one direction   this direction that never was
far from the strumming fingers   the instrument itself is music
far from the wind   salt settles into the wound of all the past
only the now is like being forgotten
lust's blank water on noon's black bed sheet
the further from blood ties the brighter it is   this instant that lights up sin
in the now there is no time   no one slowly waking
to say   illusion apart, no sea can come alive

3

無力生存的也無從挽回了

大海集體的喘息中
名字　被刨掉敏感的核
指甲抵抗著季節　謀殺徹底不朽
鳥翅搧涼了形象

誰的與被誰用一個夢做出的
停止在現在的與被停止無痛改變的
你　總是你的鏡子更邪惡的想像

缺席者更多時　更是世界
每一滴水否定著充滿視野的藍
死亡堅硬的沙子　鋪進夜晚的城市
一條新聞人物的爛魚
是骯髒的影子就一定能再次找到產婦

而誰聽見別人在耳鳴
現實才啟開　像一門最陰暗的知識

這不會過去的語言　強迫你學會
回顧中可怕的都是自己的
臉　被墓地輝映時都是鬼魂的贗品
歷史　被秋天看著就樹幹銀白
噩耗一模一樣的葉子
彼此都不是真的　卻上千次死於天空
大海　鋒利得把你毀滅成現在的你

在鏡子虛構的結局漫延無邊之處

3

alive powerless with no way to go back

in the ocean's collective panting
names   vulnerable planed-down nuts
fingernails resist the seasons   the attempt at murder is utterly immortal
bird wings have chilled the images

you are   someone's and what someone makes of a dream
what stands still and what's painlessly changed by standstill
you are   always your mirror's more vicious imagination

when more are missing   it's even more the world
each drop of water denying the blue that fills the vision
death's compacted sands   spread on night's city
the festering journalistic fish
a foul shade able again to find the woman in labour

only   when someone hears another's tinnitus
will reality open   like a syllabus of the darkest learning

this language which has no past   forces you to learn
what's fearsome when you look back is your own
face   a ghostlike fake reflected by the grave
history   the silver white of tree trunks seen by autumn
its leaves identical to the worst news of all
neither is true   yet a thousand times dying in the sky
the sea   so sharp it snuffs you out   makes you the you of this instant

where the mirror's fictive ending stretches endlessly away

大海停止之處

1

King Street　一直走
Enmore Road　右轉
Cambridge Street　14 號
大海的舌頭舔進壁爐
　　　　　　　　　一座老房子洩漏了
無數暗中監視我們的地點

我們被磨損得　剝奪得再殘破一點
影子就在地址上顯形

　　　　　　　陌生的辭僅僅是詛咒
近親繁殖的鄰居混淆著
死鴿子嘔吐出一代代城市風景
玻璃　嵌進眼球
天空　就越過鐵道驕傲地保持色盲
每個人印刷精美的廢墟的地圖上
　　　　　　　不得不擁有大海
所有不在的　再消失一點
就是一首詩　領我們返回下臨無地的家
和到處　被徹底拆除的一生

Where the sea stands still

1

King Street   straight on
Enmore Road   turn right
Cambridge Street   No.14
the sea's tongue licks into the grate
                              the old house discloses
countless places to watch us in the dark

we are so worn down   looted and left still more dilapidated
that shadows will show themselves at this address

                              unfamiliar words are only curses
                  inbred neighbours all jumbled together
            dead pigeons spew out city scenes age on age
                  glass   inlaid in eyeballs
sky   beyond the railway proudly preserves colour blindness
            a map elegantly printed with everyone's ruins
                              can't help owning the sea
            everything not there   vanishes more
is a poem   leading us back down to the house of nowhere
            and everywhere   an utterly demolished life

2

海浪的一千部百科全書打進句子
岩石刪去了合唱隊
沒有不殘忍的詩

能完成一次對詩人的探訪
寒冷　從雪白皮膚下大片溢出
灌木　引申冬天的提問

總被最後一行掏空的
遺體　總是一隻孵不出幼雛的鳥窩
一個早晨牆壁上大海的反光

讓辭與辭　把一個人醒目地埋在地下
一首詩的烏雲外什麼也不剩
誰　被自己的書寫一口口吃掉

像病人　被疾病的沉思漏掉
一部死亡的自傳　用天空懷抱死者
沒有不殘忍的美

沒有不鋸斷的詩人的手指
靜靜燃燒　在兩頁白紙間形成一輪落日
說出　說不出的恐懼

2

the thousand-part encyclopaedia of the waves hammers the sentences in
stones have deleted the choir
no poetry that isn't cruel

to finish its interview with the poet
cold   flows in clots from snow-white skin
briars   drag out winter's questioning

always picked clean by the very last line
the carcass   is always the nest where chicks cannot hatch
reflection of the sea on a morning wall

let word and word in full view bury a man below ground
nothing's left but the poem's black cloud
who   is eaten up piecemeal by his writing

like an invalid   leaks out in the brooding of his illness
the autobiography of death   embraces the dead in the sky
no beauty that isn't cruel

no poet's finger not sawn away
calmly burning   setting sun between white pages
speaking out   unspeakable fear

某個地址上　孩子切開一隻石榴
某個地址把孩子想像成
眼睛　肉裡白色的核
血　凝固成玻璃的吱吱叫的鳥兒
一半軀體在手中看不見地扭動
而牙齒上沾滿被咬破的淡紅色果凍
死　孩子看到了

那忘記我們的與被忘記無情復原的
一座入夜城市中抽象的燈火
是再次　卻絕非最後一次

剝奪我們方向的與被太多方向剝奪的
藍　總瀰漫於頭顱的高度
　　　　　　　　　在凝視裡變黑
總得有一個地點讓妄想突圍
讓構成地址的辭　瞀慣人群的潰爛

空虛　在眼眶裡
　　　　　　僅僅對稱於
大海　在瞎子們觸摸下沒有形狀

某個地址指定種植銀色幽香的骨頭
剝開我們深處
孩子被四季烘烤的杏仁
成為每個
　　　　　　想像　被看到否定的
　　　　　　被毀滅鼓舞的
石榴　裹緊藍色鈣化的顆粒
大海從未拍擊到孤獨之外
從未有別人在懸崖下粉身碎骨
我們聽見　自己都摔在別處粉身碎骨
沒有海不滑入詩的空白
用早已死亡的光切過孩子們　停止
這是從岸邊眺望自己出海之處

3

at some address   kids slice open a pomegranate
some address   imagines kids as
eyes   white nuts in flesh
blood   chirping bird congealed into glass
half a body twisting invisibly in the hands
and chewed-up pink jelly smeared on the teeth
death   kids have seen

what forgets us and what is pitilessly restored by forgetting
lamplight abstracted from a city at dusk
is again   but never for the last time

what strips us of direction and what is stripped by too many directions
blue   always unfurled in the heights of the head
blackening in a stare
must always have somewhere for vain hope to sortie out
to let the words that make addresses   get used to the pustulence of the crowd

blank   in the eye-socket
only in symmetry with
the sea   shapeless beneath blind men's hands
some address is assigned to plant silvery perfumed bones
to strip away our depths
kids   almonds roasted by the seasons
become every
imagination   denied by being seen
inspired by destruction
the pomegranate   is wrapped in blue calcified pips
the sea never yet slapped beyond solitude
never yet had another   shatter below the cliff
we hear ourselves   fall elsewhere and shatter
no sea that doesn't slip into the void of the poem
kids sliced by long-dead light   stand still   this shore
is where we see ourselves set sail

WHAUR THE
DEEP SEA DEVAULS

Whaur the deep sea devauls

1

blue's aye heicher yet   same as yir weariness
hes walit the sea   same as a bodie's glower gars the sea
get twice as dreich

gaun back same as aye
ti the wrocht stane lug whaur the drumbeats is smoorit
peerie coral corps   a yowdendrift

gairie spreckles on deid fish
same as the lift at bields yir ilka lust

gaun back ti the meiths   same as the onendin gaun back
ti the scaurs   storm heids aa about ye
yir pipes weirdit ti skirl on
efter yir daith   tunes o corruption i the howe o the flesh

whan blue's been kent at the last   the mishantert
sea   millions o caunles   blinters an devauls

2

whit's rale   lichtlies ance mair the daftness o poets
bairns gets ti shaw a jimp daith an aa
flame gars crouds o corps drap doun ti zero
ill will   hes yokit the aiss o the voar
reek sputten frae stamens   the mair quait the mair upsitten

onmellit dreidour o a wiss
this ae day   hes uised up ilka day's doul
whan fire smoors the lungs
sea bree   sees minnie's limbs stove awa in lunts
fernyear's gairden wrung out intil the sea

risin ti the zenith atween tuim skraichs o sea maas
the unleisome daiths o peerie bairns
gar daith   understudy the voar
antrin unfreinship   unfreinship o comin generations out in the derk
for refuisin ti leive i this meenit

whit's dreich an whit's dreich-like doublt   is criminal
a bodie hislane on the lip o a scaur's closer til't nor the scaur's sel
     ye're   cloured bi a thousan ton o blue stane
     een   canna jouk the deep sea's clourin
whit spies the day an whit's tirred scuddie-bare bi the day
     time   hard-core pornography for the deid

a fishbane mair shairpent yet canna weill be wrang

a drappie bluid   hes taen doun watters at oxter sunken ships
     ivorie auld-farrant an fell as a plettie
     trees   net green screeds i their beuchs ance mair

     i this snaa-white carebed   yon white is cleckin
     breists bare on riggin-heids   gells
     cheinge ilka owre-cannie haun
the lift's hurdies preined doun bi the bedheid

for the sea   the ocean skites mair senseless-like in dwaums
     clockers fykin fell like fowk

whit's past an whit's sputten out bi the past   is juist flesh
i this realitie   ye cried inti mindin   there's nocht but farawa flesh
     at wantsna blue scaurs
the sea at wantsna wings is cloured ti smush
on yir face   the leein life ilka swaw screives wi licht
     an ee starin at the scaur's lip is a caller oyster
whaur the necrosis o last nicht gangs onendinlie back

Whaur the deep sea devauls

1

on the tarrie sea a ghaist-white bird flees

reikin its road ti the shore   the lichthous sticks
at the left   airt whaur we wan til our ontimeous end

on the tarrie sea an anchor's a broken pleuch

wi the leanin o heidstanes   a hunder year
screives our names owre again
seen aside the buird o reid rock as we dine
on saut watter   green bonfire o pine needles warms an atomie
shawin a roustie-bleck mouthfu o teeth   jiggin

the wee kirk steeple staps intil this nicht ilka August
a gell   the Questions i the buik o daith

licht stops   whaur mair deid gaither
the anchor chein's snappit   anchor sunken doun whaur bairnies greit
ilka jo oxtert ticht ablow the tar

efter a hunder year we kent the bleckness o the knock

2

the fends o the flouers hae muckle seas i their sichts
a gless o beer waitin on sunset   ti pent gowd an yalla
like a dwynin ill o the lip
yon speaker   aye speakin throu the gless

yon singer   electrocutit inti sang
wi tenfauld volume ti sneck up a deefie
smile   recordit
mait   knacks fingers aff

mariners' droundit scaddows   rive on in
multiplie atween chair an chair
atween souchs wund on wund's a ramsh an saut shingle o bluid
yon ane cried a bodie   maks words rive an spleet

stane's snaw-white heel stramps on the primal grund
giein the stair o hairtbeats the pairls
the days   at gaes naither up nor doun hes wan ti
the hinnermaist   drucken   cuid-chowit   sea

3

pairlt years an years forcit in bi the pairls
years in sunken ships
flesh at mindsna hou ti baniss doul gants wide its ain skin
intimmers touched at lang an lest bi the muckle sea

the wuishen-clean liver a white lubbertie
picklt face   haudin doun stern bi the thousan
bed reivit bi a tortoise   aye blawin a sheinin horn

whaur the munelicht's nae dout our watterburn
tides   onendinlie scart younger wames clean
cries for help devaul   in ilka lug no there

i the meenit afore the shark's bluidie onset   hingin quait

we dinna flit   hotts o roust fill the lift
we're flitted   the muckle sea's purpie sheddae grips hard
on a hunder year   twae hauns slaver ink
kittle   mauchtless an mauchtlesslie gotten sleep
shame   striddlin the lichthous
kittles   the fykie flesh at deid fowk left ti the shore
wheelin birdies is tottie wee bous ti shuit at five fingers
our deid-kists canna but chase this nicht

howk it out   yon faddomless mishantert sea-graff devauls
whaur storm nor gell can niver devaul

167

Whaur the deep sea devauls

1

King Street   strecht on
Enmore Road   gang richt
Cambridge Street   No.14
the sea's tongue licks i the ingle
         the auld hous shaws
ondeemous airts ti spy us i the derk

   we're that forfochen   herried an mair disjaskit yet
    scaddows will kythe at this address

               fremmit words are nae mair nor curses
      inbred neibours aa throuither
   deid doos boke out age on age o city sichts
     gless   inlaid in the baas o the een
lift   ayont the railway hings on heid-heich ti colour-blindness
   on a map knackilie prentit wi aabodie's larachs
              canna help awnin the sea
   aathing no there   eelies faurer awa
is a poem   takin us back doun ti the hous o nae place
  an in ilka airt   a life caa'd alluterlie doun

2

the thousanfauld encyclopaedia o swaws caas the lines in
     stanes hae deletit the queir
     nae poem at isna a fell ane

     ti feinish aff its collogue wi the makar
  cauld   lappers out frae snaw-white skin
   breirs   harl out winter's speirins

     aye pykit clean bi the hinmaist line
 the corp   is aye the nest whaur younkers canna clock
    sea refleckin aff a forenoon waa

lat word an word in fair sicht yird a man ablow the mools
    naethin left bar the poem's bleck clud
   wha   is etten in smaas bi his screivin

like a bodie no weill   sypes awa wi the mumpin o his ill
daith's ain tale   oxters the deid i the lift
nae beautie at isna a fell ane

nae makar's finger no sawn awa
luntin lown   day-set atween white pages
tellin out   ontellable dreid

3

at some address   bairns spelders aipple-garnets
some address   jalouses bairns is
een   wheeplin birds jeelit inti gless
hauf a corp thrawn invisiblie atween the hauns
an pink chowit jeelie slaigert owre the teeth
daith   bairns hes seen

whit forgets us and whit's peitilesslie brocht back bi forgettin
leerie's lichts taen frae a gloamin toun
is ance mair   but niver the hinmaist time

what tirrs us o our airts an whit's tirred bi owre monie airts
blue   aye lowsed i the hichts o the heid
blecknin in a glower
maun aye hae a bit whaur wanhowp can ride a raid
ti gar the words at maks addresses   get uised wi the atter o the thrang

tuim   i the ee's hole
its ae an ane maik
the sea   formless atween blin men's hauns

some address is assignate ti plant perfumed banes o siller
ti tirr awa our deepths
bairns   almonds sneystert bi the seasons
turn ti ilka
jalousin   denied wi bein seen
upheizit wi ruin
aipple-garnets   happit wi blue caukie pips
the sea niver yet skelpit ayont solitude
niver yet hed anither   shatter ablow the scaurs
we hear oursels   faa ithergates an shatter
nae sea at disna snoove inti the tuim poem
bairns speldert bi lang-deid licht   devaul
this shore is whaur we see oursels set sail

TRANSLATING YANG LIAN

'Like MacDiarmid meets Rilke with samurai sword drawn' – W.N.HERBERT [1]

To show the stages by which I came to find an English voice for Yang Lian, this most interesting and original of contemporary Chinese poets, is to outline my own history as a translator, for the voice which I found for him is my own as much as it is his. When we discuss these English poems, Yang and I talk of them as 'ours', not 'his' or 'mine', and in fact they are a collaborative effort. Once a near-final draft has emerged, it goes back to him for a detailed reading. His comments and ideas are noted, acted on or debated, and in this way we slowly come to a final version.

Or as final as any version can be.[2] Some poems spring into life fully formed, having hardly changed at all from first to final draft, while others are the product of long reflection, months of apparent neglect in the drawer, and seemingly endless discussion. Some start life as clumsy literals, and progress smoothly through the process of turning a draft into a poem, while others stubbornly resist all our attempts to breathe them into life, until a sudden moment – epiphanic or irascible – allows the poem hidden within a limping draft to shape itself and speak. Many are, I confess, no better than they should be: like a parent inured to the unruly ways of a problem child, the translator must sometimes wash his hands of the surly poem that refuses to be beautiful, that stubbornly resists the best efforts of poet, translator and editor combined. As translators we quickly find that some the poems we deal with are self-willed and ungovernable creatures with a core that refuses to be carried over: these we can only send out into the world with our small blessing and (it has to be admitted) a rueful sigh in which relief plays some part.

Yang Lian and I share a love of some voices whose echoes may, we hope, find their way to the reader: the shades of Yeats, Rilke, MacDiarmid and Pound must be invoked here. As a translator from Chinese, Pound has been a constant inspiration for me, his felicities and lucky hits far outweighing his howlers and his extremes; Yeats and Rilke taught the marrying of complex rhythms to strange and stirring images, and for a Scottish translator, MacDiarmid bestrides the 20th century, indeed can be said to have made 20th-century Scottish writing possible (there are few works where his hand or his voice cannot be traced, even if it is only in the unspoken reaction to his dominant voice); in addition, the rhythms of MacDiarmid's voice have deeply influenced my work in both English and Scots. Important voices for Yang also include Neruda, William Carlos Williams and Charles Olsen, and these I have tried to accommodate, trying to raise the scale of my translations to those awesome heights.

Yang and I also share the vast treasure-house of Chinese literature: there are more books in Chinese than in any other language, so many that no one has ever read *all* the books. Yang is at home in this literature much more than I am, of course, and, it must be said, much more than the vast majority of his generation in China. He has steeped himself in this tradition to which I am an occasional visitor, and for a translator this raises some specific problems to which I will return: for the moment let me simply say that here are rich seams of influence, profound echoes from a long and book-haunted history which are not at all easy to carry over or impersonate. Central to his work are two voices which I have long loved: first is *Yi Jing*,[3] the ancient *Book of Change*, that vast and numinous cornucopia of images in which all creation is figured; second is the voice of Qu Yuan (?340-278 BC),[4] that elegant remonstrator of royalty who died in exile, leaving behind some hauntingly beautiful and puzzlingly obscure works which have always hovered on the edge of respectability. Both have influenced my own poetic sensibility as much as they have influenced Yang's – a convergence which makes the resonance between my voice and his all the richer.

All translators find their own voice through the medium of another author: it is the paradox of translation. We are actors, not playwrights. Though we may create a voice, we are forever speaking someone else's lines – we may speak them with passion, conviction, elegance or grace but we are play-acting, in the end. Medical translators pretend to write like doctors, legal translators like lawyers, scientific and technical translators like engineers, scientists or computer programmers, and literary translators only pretend to be poets.

In the struggle to find a voice for an author, there are more echoes than can be listed here – it could almost be said that every voice has its echo somewhere, every voice the translator has heard or read lodges itself deep in the back of the mind, and resonates in sympathy with the voice of the original text. I too have been influenced by many voices, not all of them English: Silver Latin, Classical Greek, the awesomely spare and elegant style of classical Chinese poetry and the austere yet deeply human voice of the Chinese classics; the voices of the poets of the first world war and the voices of Modernism; Lorca and Neruda and Ovid and Jin Shengtan, MacCaig and Garioch and Sorley Maclean, Swinburne and Stevenson and the Shakespeare of the Sonnets, Dunbar, Henryson, Blin Hary and Barbour, Du Fu and Li Shangyin and Bai Juyi, Confucius and Zhuangzi and Gu Yanwu, Homer, the Border Ballads, Burns, Fergusson, Scott, Hogg, *Genji no Monogatari*, Proust and – this list will never end. As long as we are reading, we are absorbing new voices, hearing and seeing new ways of speech, new gradations of language, new intricacies of thought, and all of these will, if we are attentive and if we are lucky, merge into a single voice which sings in unison with the voice of our text. So, in the end, we look for a voice – that unique combination of rhythm, image, sound structure, tone, and other near-imperceptible but essential elements which make a single voice as unique as a single face. That voice evolves over the years, as the translator gets to know the writer and the works. It evolves, too, through experiment and almost endless revision, until the translator slowly learns to sing in a kind of unison with the poet.

It's a strange business, translation. Impersonation of an author is not yet a chargeable offence in the courts of philosophy, but it's a doubtful and slippery affair. Imagine the strangeness of the relationship that has to be formed, the collusion between reader and writer complicated and compromised (sadly, always compromised) by the intrusion of the third party, the translator whose stage whisper is always there, almost audible if he's good, and crashingly, mind-numbingly obvious if he isn't.

Yang Lian has described the writing of poetry as being like 'building a tower from the top down',[5] and I agree that there is something absurd in the attempt to take a poem – in itself an attempt to subvert language, to say the unsayable – and try to re-state it in another language. At least with translation we have a scaffold on which to hang our construction, perilous and shaky though it might be.

Yang Lian's work is not difficult to translate because his language is difficult: while Chinese has some extremely recondite and obscure registers, the language Yang uses is both easily colloquial and dazzlingly precise – the difficulty comes in the strangeness of his vision and the bizarre quality of his imagination. The title of 'Dreams, or each river's third bank' encapsulates the delightful conceit that each object, every phenomenon has a component which only appears in dreaming, whether our own dreams of rivers or a river's dream of itself, and nothing can be complete without its dream-component. And in 'Crow's proposition' the line

crow uses darkness   to display light

introduces us to Yang's idea, itself as old as Chinese thought, of a kind of dynamic duality: light and dark, life and death, sea and shore, poet and reader are linked in endless tension like Yin and Yang, neither half of each pair able to exist (or be thought of) without its defining other.

The problem which Yang Lian poses for his translators[6] is that you can never second-guess a surrealist, any more than you can predict a dream. The translator must be alert to every nuance, awake to all the possibilities of interpretation in each word, each line, and each poem. And in Yang's case the unpredictability of the imagery is dizzying – when I began to work with him I was often forced to admit that, while I know perfectly well what he was saying, I was much less certain of what he meant. That problem has diminished with the years, but it will never quite go away. He remains a unique poetic voice, quite unlike his contemporaries in the precision and power of his images. In these poems the voice is never mere ranting or idle doodling, for there is, as I have written elsewhere, an urgent task involved: for Yang Lian poetry and the summoning of the poetic voice is an almost shamanistic act, involving the terrible struggle to attain a kind of Yeatsian 'mature wisdom'.[7]

Some of the poems have an autobiographical element, but it is stated so indirectly that without the author's elucidation it remains latent, implicit. 'The composer's tower', for example, draws its inspiration from an incident which took place when Yang was eleven years old, and the Red Guards came to interrogate his father. The poet himself points out that the sound of Beethoven's late quartets resonates through the entire sequence,

as negating light moves from note to note.

For a translator there are problems that relate to the experience itself: can I fully convey the terror inspired by the Red Guards, the fear and the dislocation of those ten years of chaos we call the 'Cultural Revolution', when all my experience of it is second-hand, obtained through reminiscences, books, newspapers and vaguely-remembered newsreel footage? Of course, as a child I did experience fear, and that is the common link between us: although we are divided by the specifics of our historical experience, we are united by the

175

commonality of human experience. That is a message Yang would wish his work to convey. He has written

> ...the distances between western and Chinese culture shrink into a single body – not two-dimensional, but deeply layered: not two different pieces of writing, but two editions of the same work; they don't determine me, I combine them, take them apart, restructure them, bring them into being in every poem, not just in Chinese, but in 'Yanglish' too...the only culture is my own personal culture, and the adjective 'personal' is enough to include 'Chinese', 'Western', 'traditional', modern' [8]

Turning now to the basics of language, it may be helpful to understand some of the substance of Chinese, how it functions, and how this affects the work of the translator. Chinese belongs to the same language group as English – that is to say, the great collection of languages whose simple sentences are structured *Subject-Verb-Object*, and like English, it is word order which determines sense (*man bites dog* versus *dog bites man*). Unlike English however, Chinese does not explicitly mark many of the things we take for granted in European languages – for example, tense, mood, number, gender, passive/active, definite/indefinite. There are no articles, nouns do not conjugate, verbs do not decline, and there is a general tendency towards omission and elision, especially of pronouns. So almost every instance in these translations where the words *a* or *the* appear, most pronouns, and almost every tense-marked verb (every *will*, *have* or *had*) are the result of conscious decisions by either the translator, the poet, or both. We have had to add to the sinewy grace of the Chinese these markers which clumsily insist on pinning down a poem in past, present or future, which stunt an image by squeezing it from the realm of infinite possibility into the realm of the specific, or which force statements with a universal resonance into an apparent precision which is only an illusion created by grammatical structures.

This is not to say that Chinese is a language by nature vague and incapable of precise formulation, as the semi-literate missionaries of last century asserted – don't believe that one for a minute. Chinese is just as capable of English of exactitude and precision, but it scores over English in that it is capable of more ambiguity, of multiple possibilities of interpretation – and that ambiguity, that movement in the eternal world of the image, the alternate reality of metaphor, has been lovingly cultured over three millennia of poetic expression, in a culture which has always rated poetry above all other arts. Language and poetics, culture and linguistics, acting and reacting on each other to produce a sublime balance between what is said and what is implied. *Yan wai you yi*, 'Meaning lies beyond language', as the ancient maxim has it.

While simple sentences follow the same word order as English, complex sentences have a very different form: there is a relative pronoun, but it is little used, so relative clauses are expressed by using subordinate phrases before the main headword. In English the effect would be that of rendering *The man next door who keeps pigeons* as *the next door keep pigeons man*. As a result, and particularly in cases involving enjambement, lines must often be transposed or sentences turned inside out, to allow the translation to make sense in English.

Now, since Yang uses a kind of *vers libre* which has been the standard poetic form in China since the 20s, this matters less than it would if he used a strict rhyming form. I have tried to be as precise as possible in rendering the form of the poems: almost all mid-line breaks are Yang's (in a very few cases I have added or subtracted a break, for reasons of syntax or rhythm), and wherever I can I keep to the line length he has used. He uses a sprung rhythm which transfers fairly well into English. We have read together, each taking a line at a time, and we have found that I have by and large succeeded in preserving the rhythmic structure. (Yang calls this kind of reading 'stereo poetry', and has even experimented with simultaneous reading of both Chinese and Scots versions – an effect of some power, but not one that can be used over any great length of time.)[9] Interestingly, the first time Yang and I read *Whaur the Deep Sea Devauls*[10] together – the first time he had heard the translation – he commented on how closely he felt the rhythms and textures of Scots resemble those of his own Beijing dialect, and how Scots renders the soundscape of his poetry much better than English, to his ear.

Rhyme is not a feature of Yang's poetry, but occasional alliteration is. This is something quite new in Chinese, and while Yang has experimented with poetic forms whose structure is underpinned by consonant-rhyme, none of these experimental works appear in this volume.[11] I have not tried to imitate his patterns of alliteration, but have rather tried to bring the same alliterative density to each English version as appears in the original Chinese poem.

Of all the great world languages, Chinese is the poorest in speech sounds, which makes rhyme or alliteration fairly easy. It is this paucity of speech sounds which was probably associated with the development of tones in Chinese. This requires a little explanation. Each syllable in modern Chinese has three constituents – an initial, a final and a tone. In Modern Standard Chinese[12] each syllable can be pronounced in four ways: with a high level pitch contour, a rising one, a low dipping one, or a high falling one – these are the four tones.[13] To the Chinese ear ma^1 (high level), ma^2 (rising), ma^3 (dipping) and ma^4 (falling) are as distinct as *mat, map, mad, mac* are to the English ear.

The classical poetic forms which are part an parcel of every Chinese education – especially the *shi* or 'regulated verse' which reached a glorious peak in the Tang dynasty – are built not on stress rhythms or on vowel length but on tonal patterns, and while they are not fundamental to modern poetics, there can be no denying that tonal patterns still have a great influence on the aural texture and colour of a poem. This obviously presents problems to the translator, for here is an area of language that simply cannot be carried over into a non-tonal language like English. Although in cold print I have little choice but to ignore this, anyone fortunate enough to hear Yang Lian read his own work – and he is a charismatic and compelling performer – will hear how the lilting music of the tones colours his verse.

My translation method is straightforward. First, a quick reading of the poem to establish its outline in my mind, then a more detailed look, with a Chinese-English dictionary to hand: at this point odd fragments – lines, phrases – will begin to form and are jotted in the margin. Next comes an in-depth reading with monolingual Chinese dictionaries to hand, in an effort to establish precise nuances. Then the first literal draft goes onto disk, and I move on to the next poem. At this stage I will contact Yang Lian and/or consult a native informant about any difficult words or lines. After a day or two, I will go back to the poem and attempt a first English version: this is the point at which I begin to make a poem, when I am fairly certain of the meaning, and ready to begin transforming the ugly literal into something a little more graceful. After polishing the English I will then return to the original and make a detailed comparison of Yang's text with my own, polishing for sense in an effort to ensure that I have not strayed too far from the sense of Yang's text. After that, one more look at the poetry of my draft – checking for assonances, dissonances, alliteration (intended and otherwise) and rhythm – then the draft poems will go in batches to Yang for his comments. When they return, I will give his comments a careful reading (he has saved me from many howlers) and decide which should be incorporated in the next draft. The majority of Yang's suggestions are invaluable – he is a detailed and precise critic, and will often write several sentences elucidating a single line – but there are some suggestions which are based on minor misunderstandings of my text. (Since his English is entirely self-taught – this is another sense of the 'Yanglish' he referred to above – the reading of the drafts entails a substantial amount of work on his part: in the early days of our collaboration, he would painfully go through my drafts word by word, using the dictionary to check almost every word.) I then complete a pre-final draft which is left untouched for as long as possible: the aim is to retrieve a freshness of vision when I look at my text again – this is the point at which many of my own infelicities are spotted and corrected, and a final draft emerges. Sometimes as part of this process I will hand the draft to a non-Chinese speaker for comments.[14]

So the process of reaching a final version is one of continual feedback, circling from original to draft and back again, shuffling and sorting possibilities, juggling with variants, sifting through the drafts to find the line that rings true, the phrase that speaks out, the poem that sings. Rather like Rodin's notion that the sculptor's task is to find the sculpture hidden in the stone, it often seems that the task of poetry translation is one of revelation, polishing away at the surface of a draft to reveal the poem that lies beneath it.

As for Yang Lian's own individual voice – where does that come from? How did he begin to write the way he does now? Let him speak:

> To open up language is to open up possibilities of thinking and feeling, and this is the profoundest of the poetry's themes.[15]

* * *

> From the 1980s onward I have been assessed in at least three different ways:
> – as 'a poet opposed to tradition' – when the poetry began to discover its own language, it was of course bewildering to those whose reading habits had been nurtured by Cultural revolution slogans;
> – as 'a Seeker after Roots – a poet pursuing tradition' – poem cycles of mine like *Banpo, Dunhuang*, or *In symmetry with Death* examined the history of a miserable reality, but because of their titles it was mistakenly assumed that I wanted to 'regress to a past which had once been exuberant and brilliant';
> – as 'a poet who has discarded tradition' – after 1989 I changed from being an exiled Chinese poet to a Chinese poet who wanders the world on a New Zealand passport, and who has no external proof of 'Chineseness' except his poetry, which is written in Chinese.

178

As I said to a Scottish poet who was showing me the ruins of Macbeth's castle, 'I've almost forgotten the feeling of being a poet who lives in his own country'. But did I ever have 'my own country'?[16]

* * *

...[China] is 'my own foreign land'...By any measure of significance, this is much further away than 'separation' – I have inserted an uncrossable distance between my past and my future.' [17]

* * *

On 8 August 1988 I crossed the Chinese border. In my bag was the long poem *Yi* which I had worked on for five years.[18] In its two final sections, 'Going Home' and 'Travelling Far', I had written my future like a curse:

> *we are outside ourselves*
> *and on the inside   allow a savage claw*
> *to claw bright running blood from everyone*
> *every non-person   goes home when he can't go home*

('Going home')

> *every bird escapes where   the valley of death*
> *and extends to where   this time, this place*
> *not one but ploughed a dark body*

('Travelling far')

The poem knows better than the poet what kind of reality has been apportioned to him. Because the poem already contains that reality – just as, when *Yi* was revealing itself day by day, the poems that came before it and my 33 years of life in China were its first draft; ten years of wandering abroad have preserved an orientation perpendicular to the paper: the 'I' concealed in poem after poem becomes the background to the poems. Between the words and the lines, it is both non-existent and never-vanishing. A poet always lives on (is reflected on) the other side of a pitch-black shining gravestone of marble, a phantom of flesh and blood, a shadowy authenticity.[19]

* * *

I first discovered my own language at the same time as I was discovered by plain-clothes police, police surveillance, police cars and policemen...[20]

* * *

In the 'cultural self-examination' in China in the 80s I was called a 'Roots' poet. But I am not at all like black Americans, seeking my ancestral roots on another continent. The 'roots' I seek are inside myself: the 'self' and the 'individuality' that were long ago lost in the long since sealed-off structure of Chinese society and thought – I seek a return to the ability to be aware of one's own cultural tradition.[21]

* * *

In 1987, 'Survivors' was chosen as the name of an underground poetry club in Beijing. 1989, as I discovered to my horror, turned blood-red. We were all 'survivors'. The next thing was that the facts changed the language: it was now 'survivor literature'. now that I am in the west, enforced exile has turned the motif of 'my own personal culture', a consciousness forced into shape by the realities of China, into several driving pursuits:...how to unconsciously use the 'synchronicity' of Chinese[22] to paste together ancient and modern material, in order to restructure 'my' history of China; now I am among foreign poets, it has struck me forcibly how poetry everywhere finds difficulties with language and everywhere transcends language; the pain of being unable to communicate means that my writing has completely turned back to itself – is this good luck or bad? Now, apart from the Chinese language 'I' have no background and no direction; apart from a poem, this life has neither time nor place. Poetry includes all time and place: 'I' am standing between the desolate parallel lines of where the Berlin Wall used to be, and I am curled up in a damp basement in Brooklyn; I am gazing at the distant seagulls from the cliffs above the Pacific at Sydney, and I am broke and stranded on the unbearably crowded streets of London.[23]

In 1978, along with Mang Ke, Bei Dao, Shu Ting and Gu Cheng, Yang Lian was among the founders of the literary magazine *Jintian* ('Today'). The group of young poets for whom this magazine was a focus became collectively known as the Menglong School. *Menglong* is an adjective meaning 'dim' or 'hazy', with a transferred sense of 'obscure', 'vague': it was first applied in a pejorative sense to the poetry of this school by the apparatchiks of the Party's literary wing, and soon taken over proudly by the poets themselves. As I have pointed out elsewhere,[24] the term *menglong* has been translated by Eugene Eoyang as 'Ambiguist' and by Sabina Peschel as 'Hermetic Lyricism': both translations have some value, in that they give some indication of the poetic practice of this group on the late 70s and early to mid 80s – a love of multiple meanings, and the development of a lyric poetry of an emotional subjectivity pushed to the limits of intelligibility.

Young people of this generation had had their lives disrupted by the ten years of the Cultural Revolution, their education had been suspended, they had been sent down to the countryside for 're-education', and as a result they shared a profound distrust of authority, of politics, and of accepted truth. Their weapons in their fight against the established order were language, which they pushed to its limit in search of deeply-felt but unsayable truths, and metaphor, which they saw as an alternate universe, or a way of transcending the bounds of a materialistic 'reality' imposed on personal subjectivity by the official creed of the Communist Party. Their project was nothing less than the re-discovery of the self and the re-invention of Chinese culture.

During the mid-80s this was poetry as popular as rock music, poetry which changed the lives of the young students who memorised and quoted it incessantly, and the poets were (and often still are) idolised by their readers. The poets were also subject to savage attacks from the official media, their works were often banned, or circulated in *samizdat* editions, and since the late 80s, all the surviving members of the group are in exile or no longer writing poetry. Yang Lian, after spending almost ten years drifting from New Zealand through Australia, Germany, and the USA, now lives in exile in London, unable to return to China officially. The only active member of the group left in Beijing is Mang Ke, who has given up writing poetry, concentrating instead on encouraging younger writers and on writing fiction.[25] Gu Cheng died by his own hand in New Zealand in 1995. Bei Dao has retreated into smaller poetic spaces, creating an inward and private verse of a more intimate and less exploratory kind.

Yang, on the other hand, has created a poetic style of extraordinary grandeur. Of *Where the Sea Stands Still*, the sequence that is the climax of this collection, he writes:

> ...[the] ever-moving sea stands still in the midst of its restlessness; it is here in the midst of nowhere; and in the space of the poem, time is swept away. Because of Odysseus, the sea began its endless ebb and flow; when this sequence was written, the sea stood still, and became an illusion.[26]

This breathtakingly audacious piece is an extended meditation on time (*the hard-core pornography of the dead*), reality (*a syllabus of the darkest learning*) and the nature of consciousness. It was conceived in a moment when Yang was sitting below a cliff near Sydney, watching the ocean: in that moment, for him the sea stood still, and the poem cycle is an attempt to transmit or evoke that moment. For Yang poetry must be ruthless in its attempt to strip away the accretions of habit and illusion which bind us to the familiar but ultimately unreal world we inhabit:

> *no poetry that isn't cruel*

and, because of its ultimate irreality, so too,

> *no beauty that isn't cruel.*

The notion is one that is familiar from Buddhist philosophy, of course. To Buddhists this world, however tragically beautiful it may be, is not the ultimate reality, for all we know of it comes from the evidence of our senses: 'illusion' in Buddhist thinking is the result of relying on the evidence of sense-perception. This idea of a separate self, which creates and acts as the root of illusion, is produced by the apparently continuous nature of sense-perception. 'Reality', if such a word means anything at all, is to be found elsewhere, through meditation, and the realisation of the essential oneness of all phenomena; 'reality' is what fills the spaces between sub-atomic particles or between stars; 'reality' may be called 'mind' or it may be called 'love', but in practice the distinction is immaterial, because words are inadequate to describe the seamless oneness of true 'reality'. The Upanishads say:

> *word and mind go to him but reach him not and return.*[27]

Yang does not describe himself as a Buddhist ('I like the philosophy, but not the church', he said to me one day), but Buddhism does provide a useful avenue for approaching his more philosophical poems, where the sense of self and the evidence of sense-perceptions are in question.

Underlying the poem, too, is an ancient Chinese idea: 'stillness in motion, and motion in stillness: that is the numinous'.[28] For many of the ancient philosophers of the Spring and Autumn (770-476 BC) and Warring States (475-221 BC) periods, reality could only be described through the observation of the interaction of opposing principles. Hence for Yang '...[the] ever-moving sea stands still in the midst of its restlessness', and in the paradox of the unity of motion and stillness, time stands still:

> *in the now there is no time   no one slowly waking*
>
> *to say   illusion apart, no sea can come alive.*

The book as a whole is made up of different sections: *Darknesses* was written in New York in the spring of 1992, *House Like Shadow* at Yaddo, NY in the summer of that year; *The Sky Shifts* was written in Auckland, New Zealand in the summer of 1992, while *Pomegranates Denied* and *Where the Sea Stands Still* were written in Sydney, Australia from late 1992 to mid-1993. The sections alternate in form:

> *Darknesses* is a poem cycle which acts as a preface to the collection; *House Like Shadow* is a collection of short poems; *The Sky Shifts* is a cycle of medium-length poems using long lines, with relatively slow and deliberate rhythms; *Pomegranates Denied* consists of a collection of short poems with skipping and irregular rhythms; *Where the Sea Stands Still*, the culminating point of my short poems, returns to the idea of 'spatial structure', taking to an extreme the themes of drifting and of endings, bringing to an end both the book and my own experience [of these themes]...[29]

Yang goes on in this essay to explain how he sees the structure of the poem cycle:

> I see *Where the Sea Stands Still* as a single unit because, while it is the climax [of this collection], it is also the beginning of another stage – that of 'spatial poems'. It is included in this collection of short poems because of its structure, made up as it is of twelve poems arranged in four sections...each poem can be seen as separate and independent, the structure and style of each collectively representing the characteristics of my short poems, but the twelve taken as a whole are united by a common conception and a unified overall structure. Taken as a whole it reproduces the theme of 'intelligent space' which I have been using for the last ten years. In my wanderings after *Yi*, I once again began to use the concept of 'space': the four sections are like four independent sonatas, each made up of poems numbered 1, 2 and 3. In each, poem 1 states the theme (as in the [implicit] theme of 'endings' in the first section), while poem 3 echoes, develops and completes this theme; poem 2, though, is an independent poem (a digression) concerned with the *external surface* of the theme. If you look at the four sections together, then you will see the whole of *Where the Sea Stands Still* is a symphony. The four movements intensify, layer by layer, and are intentionally 'overlapping' in form [linked by devices such as] the title *Where the Sea Stands Still* which precedes each section; the grammatical structures used in each poem 3 (e.g. *what's drab and what's drably copied, what's past and what's spat out by the past* etc.); the use of the preposition 'where' in the final line of each section, and so on. This sets up echoes repeated through the whole poem which deepen layer by layer until the four poems of *Where the Sea Stands Still* stop at one point – NOW. And the illusion of the 'now' includes at every level time, life, language, history... even this person at this address. There is no place which is not abstract, and there is no illusion which is not manifest in this life at this moment – now is furthest away, but at the same time, there is only one 'now'.[30]

Whaur the Deep Sea Devauls, my Scots version of *Where the Sea Stands Still*, is included at Yang Lian's request as another take on the same poem sequence, which he felt was important enough to be read in more than one version. Indeed, he feels that it is the most important piece he has written in the ten years since he left China.

In performance *Where the Sea Stands Still* is startling: the wave-like rhythms of the piece, and the regular recurrence of image piled upon image, produce a hypnotic effect: Yang has written that

> Each of my poems is a mandala. Each poem passes through different levels of change and development to become a self-sufficient linguistic universe...as with music, several motifs will be developed and varied...and at the highest level they will converge.[31]

Like a mandala, the poem is intended to point the way to a higher level of awareness, a deeper sense of how we apprehend our world. Like Qu Yuan before him, and like the earliest strata of the *Yi Jing*, there is something shamanistic about this aspect of Yang's work. Rhythm, image, tone colour and sense combine to lead the reader or (even better) the listener through the dream-like labyrinth of the poem into a sense of halted time, a moment where the restless sea does indeed stand still:

> this shore is where we see ourselves set sail.[32]

Unsettling and unexpected images are presented with a dazzling virtuosity: to take a single instance, the act of drinking a glass of beer on a summer evening is transmogrified into something strangely sinister:

> a beer glass waits for sunset   to paint gold and yellow
> like a steadily sinking disease on the lips.

There is a dream-like, surreal quality to the way that images develop, recur and resonate through the poem cycle, and through the collection as a whole.

In all of Yang's work, the sense of self, the nature of reality and of time, and the ever-present world of dreams are continually raised and questioned, where, like Qu Yuan, *'the madman's only mistake/ is to be always waking'* ('Ark'). Behind the façade of everyday life, the poet sees the illusion of self, as in 'Neighbours', where the domestic scene of a suburban barbecue is presented in hallucinatory detail, warped out of normal vision to reveal the horrors that lurk beneath the surface: what is it that lies cobwebbed in the attic? what is *'the shame we all should feel'*? why is it that *'to be forgotten is good fortune'*?

Death is with us all through these poems, the silent witness of the strangeness of our lives.

> yes   death the mother-like eye
> has perfumed the tree
> it's death in a mother's eye that gives birth to a poem of summer
> this purple flower has bloomed all the way to your end
> reflection of pure black marble   makes you die at your start
>
> ...
>
> you are hopelessly born from the death in your own eyes
> ('The shape of ghosts')

Death is the defining factor. Without death there is no meaning in life. Without death we have no way of knowing we are alive. In this equation there is hope, there is clarity, and there is a lyrical elegance, as in 'The simplest thing', which had its genesis in a television documentary which showed the death of a guinea-pig attacked by piranhas:

> a piranha bares a mouthful of smiling teeth
> but the moon   like a shot jailbreaker
> dies face down
>
> tear off light from shade
> from light   tear off this guinea-pig inveigled by the light
>
> the river has been raging
> four little legs   white bones all that's left of the desperate paddling
> the last skin of blood tightly clasps its body
> eyes still stare at the sky   not knowing who's eating it alive

Or 'Portrait of a medieval saint', another short reflective lyric, in which the acceptance of death is positive, life-enhancing, life affirming:

> calm acceptance of death happened long ago
> when a name cancels out a kind of wisdom
> flesh   accepts at last the gold of suffering
>
> every infant learns how to use weeping
> to dispute whether the philosophies of night
> are always more than nights themselves
>
> a requiem can't sing what is beyond wounds
> nor brushstrokes paint
> the indecent exposure of the eyes
>
> the profound sky permits no falling into it
> since then   what we have invented
> is only the redundant distance between ear and eye

Death, because it is continually defining life (like the mould that defines the brick) becomes a source of strength for Yang, a paradoxically vivifying and enriching force, which can even defy time:

> and with musical instruments death says
> rivers that give up crying for help   run back to become this silence
> run back into this instant   children climb on green benches
> wooden stakes slapped into flower again by nanny ocean
> spring   spring is lined up trim and spruce
> you've already died   so you're not afraid to love
> ('Requiem, or river running back')

Time has meaning, one the one hand, in that it represents death for us, and on the other, as the present moment. Only this present moment is real for Yang – past and future are abstractions, stories, dreams: this theme echoes and re-echoes throughout the collection.

> that's right   this summer is your summer
> on the red platform what's immortal is only one explanation
> the rusty train doesn't have to arrive
> ('Dismal summer')

In 'The shore of time', which is the culmination of the sequence *The Sky Shifts*, the theme continues: time is perceived as a closed system where '*eyes that see time see a window nailed shut*'. But if we can '*visualise one drop of water flow impossibly into another*' – a lovely variation on the idea of *nirvana*, where the self purged of the illusion of separateness slips into union with the seamless garment of Reality with all the ease of a raindrop falling into the ocean – then we will see that

> like shadow   stripped from a treetrunk lit by the sunlight
> ...no one also has a shadow.

On our journey to the shores of time across the illusory ocean of birth and death, the 'bitter sea' of Buddhist belief, there is always the possibility that we can come to a moment of realisation, of full awareness, where

Awakening from dreams or awakening into dreams, the point is to live in the present moment only – there is no other choice.

Though there is much darkness in these poems, there is also the light that shines within darkness, displayed or hinted at in beautiful images of space and light.

birds feverishly push the air aside
the sea's sighing surface   clear sinuous glass
('Space')

on the little lake the watersnakes come and go
she stands on the bank   is moonlight unconcerned with itself
('Neighbours III')

light builds its temple   with erect pillars one by one
light carves words on the dull brown stone
('Prison island')

we misremembered   the salty smells of the sea-wind every day
being bodies without an address
static motionless blue   dazzles only after memory's editing
('Biography V')

In a recent essay where he discusses his poetic practice, Yang Lian begins by saying, 'My German translator[33] said "I hate translating Yang Lian's poetry. It's just too difficult". Thanks a lot, old friend. That makes me very very happy – what if you had said "Translating your poetry is really easy"?' He ends with this: 'No, you're too kind, old friend. My poetry isn't nearly difficult enough.'[34]

In this essay Yang insists, as he always has done, that he is working within the Chinese tradition, a living tradition that is forever re-inventing itself. This is not a question of slavishly following ancient models, for the contemporary Chinese poet must be aware of other traditions, always alert for new ideas and techniques which can be adapted to enrich the tradition of which he or she is a part:

> ...'leaving' and 'returning' [to the tradition] are as necessary to each other as inhaling and exhaling. Contemporary experience gives us a sense of distance, and stimulates us to realise what has always been implicit, yet never fully revealed, in the Chinese language. This includes learning western techniques – and not simply transplanting them, for they must be absorbed into the language which we create.[35]

He continues with the question of the relationship of poetic form to content, and issue which has been debated in China for many centuries, and which still continues to exercise poets:

> 'The vexed question of 'pure poetry' has never been a problem to genuine poets: because of the expressive nature of language, there is no such thing as 'pure poetry'. But no matter what the content of your verse, as you write it you must think of it as 'pure poetry' – seeking rhythms, structures, musicality, balance and movement, precision and harmony, tension in space, and so on. Where 'Chineseness' manifests itself is in the 'pure poetry' of the formal elements. A polished poem continuously

seeks, as with every poem, to invent its 'own' form. Take as an example Qu Yuan's Questions to Heaven, Encountering Sorrow or The Nine Songs,[36] where the relation between style and content are like those between geography and landscape. Not the 'optimum', but the 'only' way, even the 'necessary' way. All great poetry, ancient or modern, Chinese or western, refuses translation or exegesis, thereby proving its own 'necessity'.[37]

Ignoring the problematic nature of this last statement for the translator (while recognising the exasperating, if partial, truth of it), we will follow Yang's argument a little further: he goes on to discuss the nature of the Chinese writing system, and how it has formed the poetic sensibility of Chinese poets. Chinese characters each represent a syllable; while there are of course monosyllabic words, the majority of the vocabulary of Chinese is made up of bisyllabic compound words (many formed on the *black+bird* = *blackbird* principle). The writing system works much like numerals do, in that each graphic character conveys sense while conveying little or no phonetic information, and just as a telephone number can be read in any language, so the characters can be read in Mandarin, Cantonese, Hakka etc (or even in Japanese, Korean or Vietnamese). There is also a graphic dimension, a visual excitement to the written language which alphabetic scripts can never convey. Virtuoso poetic exercises have been composed in which one graphic element powers the poem and almost subliminally introduces a tone or a theme which is otherwise left unstated: for instance, a poem could be written which never mentions water, yet by making judicious and subtle use of characters which contain the 'water' element, it could convey to the reader a powerful sense of chilly dampness.

> 'As a sculptor or an architect must reach the highest level of tacit understanding of his materials, so how can we come to our own unique understanding of each of these slippery, highly-polished characters, how do we retain their expressiveness and their communicative power? This is a question of the highest order for every poet.[38]

He then goes on to quote from the great Tang dynasty poet Du Fu (712-770), who is often regarded as the finest of all poets in the long Chinese tradition: he quotes the second couplet of 'Spring view' ('Chun wang'), which I give in full here, in Gary Snyder's translation:

> *The nation is ruined   but mountains and rivers remain.*
> *This spring the city   is deep in weeds and brush.*
> *Touched by the times   even flowers weep tears.*
> *Fearing leaving   the birds tangled hearts.*
> *Watch-tower fires   have been burning for three months*
> *To get a note from home   would cost ten thousand gold.*
> *Scratching my   white hair thinner*
> *Seething hopes   all in a trembling hatpin.* [39]

'*Touched by the times   even flowers weep tears / Fearing leaving   the birds tangled hearts*'. The power of the auditory rules of classical poetry is still an inspiration to us.[40] Compared to the alphabetic scripts of Europe where the sounds of the language are 'visible', the musicality of Chinese is concealed behind the visual image. Yet, because of that concealment, the effect is all the more powerful. I call it a 'secret energy'. Having left the collective support-system of classical metrics, contemporary Chinese…has lost its musicality:

fuqin   cong yinianzhong qiexia zhe zui heide yige yue
yiyue   muqinmen mangmuzhong yi xiawu yinyue [41]

('January for the Dead')

> This isn't just a simple use of parallelism, but the use of harmony and variation of sound. Contemporary poetry has given the ancient feeling of 'moulding' the music of poetry back to the poets themselves, allowing you to find the Mallarmé, the Li Shangyin [42] or the Li He [43] within yourself – so how do you draw out the flow of images and meaning from your inner ear to let other ears hear as though they listened to the voice that whispers in their dreams?' [44]

Yang next explains why, over the last ten years and more, he has taken to writing poem cycles: these include the book-length *Yi* referred to above, the cycle *Where the Sea Stands Still* which is the climax of this collection, and the new book-length cycle *Concentric Circles*, which he has recently finished, and on which he has worked for the last three years. [45]

> 'In fact, what really excites me is structure – endlessly making a frame for the living flux of sensations and feeling, in order to transfigure that flux, and at the same time stimulating language to open itself out through the contrasts, the conflicts and the resonances within the form of the poem cycle. This might be simply defined as a kind of poetic consciousness: building poetic space. Beginning from the sense of space in a work, and moving through the connections between the images, the lines, or those within one poem and between all the poems, to build the metaphor which underlies the work as a whole. I have come to understand, after a long period of trial and error, that the intuitive feel for spatial form comes from the poet's imaginative grasp of musical form... I hope that these poem cycles which present the complexities of my life have the same clarity and self-sufficiency that individual [Chinese] characters do. In themselves they are progressive layers of 'concentric circles' leading me to where we see ourselves set sail...
>
> In the final analysis, the poetic forms which are deeply implanted in the Chinese language are not limited to opening out onto contemporary human consciousness, but can open up that contemporary human consciousness itself. When the legendary inventors of the New Culture Movement created the words for time and space (*shi-jian* and *kongjian*) out of *shi* and *kong*, what changes did that make to our existence? [46] ...Beginning from the Chinese language we can reveal cultural resources that make it different to other languages, and these are no inventions. For instance, there is the magic of the Chinese verb: no matter what changes of person or tense are made, it retains its form throughout, as stable as gold. In this way that 'specificity' which the grammar of European languages tries so hard to catch is discarded at a stroke. Every action is placed in a context. Every context contains all actions that ever existed. Is this illusion or reality? Or illusion disclosing reality?......A 'synchronous' language can more thoroughly build a poetic space in order to delete time...' [47]

Finally, Yang takes up the theme of what is and what is not translatable in poetry, making the point along the way that there is an intimate relation between the success or failure of poetic translation and the translator's own skills as a poet:

> I call Pound's translations of classical Chinese poetry 'majestic misunderstandings'. These misunderstandings refreshed twentieth-century English poetry on the one hand, and on the other took such a completely new angle on Chinese that some Chinese poets are still bragging about it to this day. But don't forget that it was the brilliance of the 'Chineseness' in ancient Chinese poetry which made those 'majestic misunderstandings' possible. THE MISUNDERSTANDING WAS WORTH IT. [48]

Clearly, great poets such as Ezra Pound can produce great poetry even when they have little knowledge of the language of the original: Pound was working through Ernest Fennellosa's notes on Japanese readings of classical Chinese poetry,[49] supplemented by some rather half-baked notions of his own about the nature of the Chinese writing system. Some of his versions rest on howlers that would bring a blush to the undergraduate cheek – yet how many undergraduates could come so close to the core of the poems as Pound did? Equally, Hugh MacDiarmid's knowledge of Russian was slight, yet working through English versions he produced Scots versions of Blok, Pasternak and others which stand comparison with the best. The essential 'untranslatability' of poetry is a literary myth of long standing, and too often promulgated by translators whose talents might be thought to lie closer to linguistics than to poetry.

I have written on this subject elsewhere:

> If you choose a text from a distant time or place, you've already chosen your world as you read it, as you silently collude with the authorial voice to make it all new again – each reader has a different text, each re-reading changes the text. Then if you choose to translate the text into another medium, you create another text whose relationship with the ur-text bears some relationship to the author-reader collusion, filtered through the medium of the translator's voice. And the translator – ventriloquist and dummy together – must let his text speak in the best way he knows how.
>
> Ego is not a factor here, as the voice of the translator is not the point. The authorial voice and the translator's voice must sing together in a kind of unison, neither wholly obscured by the other, each separate and distinct, but both sharing the same modes of delight...
>
> Every act which involves the transfer of thought/emotion/sensation into language is an act of translation, and though the hidden springs of the process may not make it appear so to us, that transfer involves huge resources of brainpower: imagination, intuition, comparison, analysis, are all parts of this process. To translate a work of imagination from one tongue to another requires these same stupendous resources to be used to the full, and to be used in a conscious, directed way.
>
> It is, they say, impossible.[50]

Yet we do it, do it all the time. Of course, it's nonsense to say that poetry is impossible to translate. I have hoped to show some of the problems that beset the translator of Chinese poetry, but I hope also that the poems in this book will convince readers that much of the power and passion of this strange poetry can be captured in English, and that much can be carried over from the astonishingly creative world of modern Chinese poetry. Yang Lian is, for my money at any rate, the finest Chinese poet of his generation, and though he has been translated into many languages and has been feted in much of Europe and Asia, he remains relatively unknown in the English-speaking world.

It is my hope that this volume will help in some small way to change that: he is a unique voice, and one that deserves our attention – not because in some way we might "understand China", as the politicians would have it, but because as a poet of international stature, he speaks to the world. He does not "speak for China" any more than Shakespeare spoke for England alone, or than Yeats spoke for Ireland – like them, he speaks for himself, for us all and to us all. He speaks with the stature of a Neruda or a Rilke and, in my opinion, he stands comparison with the greatest writers of his or any other culture.

A writer's closest readers are always his translators, for we must struggle with the complexities and ambiguities of the text in a way which few other readers do. We don't do it for gain or for glory, for the material rewards are few (we also go uncredited too often, preterite and fugitive creatures that we are). No, we do it for the same reason the poet writes, we do it because we can do no other. Imagine the joy of discovering a poet who speaks directly to you across whatever distances of time and space, a poet who changes your life, and then imagine the feeling of knowing that not one of those around you has ever heard that unique voice, and never will unless you take on the task of making that poet sing in another language. There is a deep and resonant joy in the task, the joy of realising that – not always, not often, but once in a while – you have found an almost perfect form of words to render a line or a lyric. You see your poem spread its wings and set sail. That is why we do it, that joy, and the joy of knowing that not only have we made a unique voice, but we have also made that voice available to a wider world.

TRANSLATOR'S ACKNOWLEDGEMENTS

This book has been several years in the making: its appearance would have been sooner had it not been for the fact that, like most of my fellow translators, I am distracted from the work in hand by the need to make a living. Along the way there have been many who helped in its gestation: these I thank below, with the the caveat that for every translator there are also unseen voices and unremembered conversations which have all gone to swell the stream – conversations overheard, from which the mot juste has fortuitously emerged, voices on radio or TV half-heard and often totally misinterpreted in order to hear the solution to that tricky line that is lying around worrying me, apparently frivolous conversations in the pub from which the perfect singing line appears. All unaware, many people have contributed to this work, and I gratefully bear witness to them here.

I would specifically like to thank my brother Harvey Holton, John Thor Ewing, W.N. Herbert, Francis R. Jones and Lisa Raphals for their advice, comments, suggestions and interest: without any of them, this work would contain fewer poems and more tin-eared cribs. Thanks must also go to my wife, Guo Ying, and to Liu Ting-Kun, the best of friends, for helping me to avoid howlers. Thanks too to Chen Ching-Yen, Chu Hwa-Lin and Lu Shu-Ling for their willing and timely help with the Chinese texts of these poems.

As always, the greatest thanks are due to Yang Lian himself, for his unfailing helpfulness and his long-suffering patience, and to his wife You You for her encouragement and advice. Thank you, friends.

Thanks are also due to the WellSweep Press, who published the sequence *Where the Sea Stands Still* as a pamphlet in 1995.

And as is traditional, but no doubt necessary, I must remind readers that there are no error-free translations under the moon. This work of mine is not and cannot (such is the nature of the beast) be perfect. Whatever errors there are, they are mine and no one else's, and I accept responsibility for them with all the humility at my disposal.

BRIAN HOLTON

Notes

1. On *Where the Sea Stands Still* (London: WellSweep Press, 1995), which W.N. Herbert chose as poetry book of the year (*The Scotsman*, 30 November 1996).

2. Readers familiar with WellSweep Press's *Where the Sea Stands Still* will notice a few minor revisions which were made especially for this volume at Yang Lian's request.

3. Many translations are available: the most widely known is Carey Baynes' version of Richard Wilhelm's German text, which is inaccurate and often misleading. There are several more recent versions which are more reliable guides to the content of this astonishing text.

4. For a superb translation of the works ascribed to Qu Yuan, see *Songs of the South* (tr. David Hawkes, Penguin Classics, rev. edn. 1989).

5. Personal communication, 19 June 1998.

6. By his own reckoning Yang's work has now been translated into more than twenty languages.

7. *Non-Person Singular* (London: WellSweep, 1994), p.120.

8. *'Starting From My Last Day On Earth'* (Frankfurt: *Lettre*, 1998).

9. This at the première of my Scots version of the cycle, *Whaur the Deep Sea Devauls*, reading with Harvey Holton at the Netherbow, Edinburgh Festival Fringe, 1996.

10. At Morden Tower, Newcastle, November 1996.

11. In this area he acknowledges the influence of Harvey Holton's alliterative verse-forms, which were developed out of verse-forms from the medieval bardic traditions of Scotland and Ireland.

12. i.e. Mandarin, the official language of the People's Republic of China and of Taiwan.

13. Other "dialects" of Chinese – it might be more correct to call them "Chinese languages", since they are mutually unintelligible in speech – have more: Wu and Yue have five tones, and Cantonese seven or eight, for example.

14. W.N. Herbert, Francis R. Jones and John Thor Ewing have been enormously helpful in this respect.

15. 'Poet Without a Nation', *Index on Censorship*, 26 (March 1997), p.155.

16. 'Poet Without a Nation', pp.152-3.

17. *'Starting From My Last Day on Earth'*.

18. Mabel Lee's translation of *Yi* is soon to be published by Sun & Moon Press, Los Angeles.

19. *'Starting From My Last Day on Earth'*.

20. *'Starting From My Last Day on Earth'*.

21. *'Starting From My Last Day on Earth'*.

22. Yang here is referring to the fact that the Chinese language does not insist on explicit tense-markers.

23. *'Starting From My Last Day on Earth'*.

24. *Non-Person Singular* (London: WellSweep, 1994), p.123.

25. After the success of his first novel *Ye Shi* ('Screwing Around'), he is rumoured to be writing a second, satirising the emergent Beijing *nouveau riche*.

26. *Where the Sea Stands Still*, tr. John Cayley.

27. *The Upanishads*, tr. Juan Maspero (Penguin, various editions).

28. I have been unable to source this quotation (it is widely used for calligraphy scrolls and suchlike purposes), but I believe it may originate from one of the vast number of commentaries on *Yi Jing*.

29. *Structuring Poetic Space to Open Up Possibilities for Life*, unpublished MS (1995), p.4.

30. *Structuring Poetic Space*, p.7.

31. Personal communication, 23 March 1993.

32. In November 1996, my brother Harvey Holton, Yang and I gave a reading in the McManus Gallery, Dundee, where we read *Where the Sea Stands Still* and *Whaur the Deep Sea Devauls* in a trilingual English-Chinese-Scots performance for the first time. The effect was astounding, for readers and audience alike. It was an unforgettable, electrifying experience.

33. Wolfgang Kubin.

34. *Inside Chinese*, unpublished MS (9 November 1997).

35. *Inside Chinese*.

36. See Note 4 above

37. *Inside Chinese*.

38. *Inside Chinese*.

39. V. Mair (ed.), *The Columbia Anthology of Traditional Chinese Literature* (New York: Columbia University Press, 1994), p.208. For other excellent translations of Du Fu, see David Hinton (tr.), *The Selected Poems of Tu Fu* (London: Anvil Press, 1989).

40. i.e. the metrical form is based around patterns of "level" and "oblique" tones. In modern Mandarin, this couplet is read *gan shi, hua jian lei/hen bie, niao jing xin*. In the reconstructed Middle Mandarin of the period, it would have been read something like *kam zhi, hua tsien lui/ hen biet, tieu kiang siem*. See P. Demieville, *Anthologie de la poesie chinoise classique* (Paris: Gallimard, 1962). Its tonal pattern (where L = level tone and O = oblique tone and a comma marks the caesura) is $L\ L,\ L\ O\ O/O\ O,\ O\ L\ L$: such tonal parallelism, used in conjunction with grammatic and semantic parallelism, forms the backbone of classical metrics.

41. *father   cut this darkest January out of one year/January   the music of the afternoon in the blind eyes of mothers*: I give the transliteration in the text because Yang is talking about the sounds of the language here. In the standard *Hanyu Pinyin* transliteration, *Q* is pronounced like *ch*, *C* like *ts*, *X* like a light *sh*, and *ZH* like *dj*.

42. Tang dynasty poet, ?813-858

43. Tang dynasty poet, 791-817

44. *Inside Chinese*.

45. I have already begun work on this translation.

46. The early decades of this century saw the re-invention of the Chinese language, with a wholesale invention of modern "scientific" terms: *shi* and *kong* in the old written language were always intelligible as meaning "time" and "space", if capable of some ambiguity. The language was re-invented on the base of the colloquial tongue, and the language loosely and somewhat inaccurately called Classical Chinese ('Literary Chinese' would be a better term) was abandoned in favour of what we now call Modern Standard Chinese.

47. *Inside Chinese*.

48. *Inside Chinese*.

49. Which is why we meet authors such as Li Bai transmogrified into Rihaku, or Tao Yuanming appearing as To Emmei: these are the Japanese readings of the characters used on the authors' names, and Pound did not know enough at that point to give the original Chinese readings of the names.

50. 'Wale a Leid an Wale a Warld: Shuihu Zhuan into Scots' in W. Findlay (ed.) *Frae Ither Tongues: Essays on Modern Translations into Scots* (Aberdeen: Scottish Cultural Press, forthcoming).

Printed in the USA
CPSIA information can be obtained
at www.ICGtesting.com
JSHW012016140824
68134JS00025B/2451